Victoria's Empire

Victoria's Empire

Victoria Wood,
Fanny Blake and Frank Welsh

Photography by Ben Warwick

an I M G media company

HODDER &
STOUGHTON

Hodder & Stoughton
Copyright © 2007 by Tiger Aspect Productions

First published in Great Britain in 2007 by Hodder & Stoughton
A division of Hodder Headline

A Hodder & Stoughton Book

This is an account of the trips taken by Victoria Wood with Tiger Aspect
Productions for the BBC series *Victoria's Empire*. The countries are all
described in the original order they were visited in.

1

A CIP catalogue record for this title is available from the British Library

ISBN 978 0 340 938010

Book design by Janette Revill
Typeset in Adobe Minion and ITC Legacy Sans

Printed and bound by Clays Ltd, St Ives plc

Hodder Headline's policy is to use papers that are natural, renewable
and recyclable products and made from wood grown in sustainable forests.
The manufacturing processes are expected to conform to the
environmental regulations of the country of origin.

Hodder & Stoughton Ltd
A division of Hodder Headline
338 Euston Road
London NW1 3BH

Contents

Introduction   vii

1. Ghana   1

2. Jamaica   34

3. Newfoundland   63

4. India   87

5. Hong Kong   126

6. Borneo   153

7. New Zealand   180

8. Australia   215

9. Zambia   250

A Final Word   277

Introduction

Blame my mother. I think most of us can use that as an opening sentence. My mother, television-hater, uprooter of rhododendrons, collector of minor Victorian novels and planks from building sites, named me after Queen Victoria.

My childhood home, which was a massive bungalow in the Rossendale valley, partitioned at random by my mother in a series of rage-fuelled DIY escapades, was stuffed with books on Queen Victoria. I can't say they caught my interest particularly – the house was stuffed with so much else: sacks of shoe lasts, a comprehensive selection of rusty 1950s Thermos flasks, violins, complete sets of costumes from amateur productions of *The Maid of the Mountains*. So Queen Victoria was neither here nor there, a bit like my father.

But I liked my name. I thought it went well with 'Wood'. I was a bit offended when, during some reluctant but necessary appearance I was making on Radio 4's *Start the Week* in about 1975, a political commentator with dandruff and halitosis said it sounded like a stop on the Northern Line. To which I should have replied, 'At least I know how to brush my teeth, you arse!' I didn't, of course, being young and shy and in need of the thirty quid I got for playing some mediocre topical song at the piano while everyone else on the programme nipped to the lavvy.

So, fast forward thirty-odd years, whizzing by my career in stand-up comedy, the births of my two children, my triumphs on the tombola at their junior school, and cast me up on the shores of 2005 (I think – without the assassination of a president or a World Cup win it's hard to nail down the exact date) when a nice lady from a production company came to me and said did I want to go to lots of places called after Queen Victoria.

Ooh, yes, please. I did want to go to places called after Queen Victoria. It sounded fun and interesting and a lot better than most of the jobs of that sort I'd been offered. Please don't think I'm 'bigging myself up', as we say in the grocer's, when I mention I've been offered a lot of reality shows, a lot of travel programmes, and lately, a lot of *Celebrity What Not to Wear* and *Celebrity You Are What you Eat* style shows. It doesn't work for everybody, but my view is, career wise, *You Are What you Turn Down*, and that's kept me out of a whole heap of trouble.

It's quite dispiriting to get a fax from your agent saying, 'Would you like to be considered for *Ten Years Younger/How Clean Is Your House?*' Who do they think I am? Quentin Crisp? My house is very clean, and if I was ten years younger I'd have missed out on hot-pants so leave me be.

When the first series of *I'm a Celebrity Get Me Out of Here* was being planned I did give it a passing thought – it sounded challenging and a teeny bit dangerous. How were we to know it would end up as a lot of not-very-well-known whingers chomping bits of wallaby sphincter in an attempt to land a job advertising sofas? But Ant and Dec, I have to say – I've been on their Saturday-morning show – are charming. And I worked out a good way to remember which was which – it's simply that Ant, the dark one, is a tiny bit like a very good-looking ant. You look, next time he's on. You'll never get them mixed up again.

I was never tempted by *Big Brother*, which always seemed to me to combine the worst elements of cocktail parties and youth-hostelling – namely, a lot of rubbish being talked plus having to endure other people's idiosyncratic ideas on teabag disposal.

Ballroom dancing and ice skating both had to get the thumbs-down. I'd love to learn to dance – who wouldn't want to be cracking some tricky rhumba manoeuvre, with a sweat darkened ponytail and some neat jazz pants, perhaps slamming out of the rehearsal room once in a while, begging brusquely for 'Just a minute, OK?' while some baffled Adonis shrugs and picks a bit of fluff off a honed glute? I'd love to do all that, just not on television.

Ice skating . . . I love the cold, I love moving about, I love the knitwear, I love the whole Central Park fairy-lights outdoorsy aspect of it – it's the staggering around on knife blades, hurty ankles, 'She never really got over the pelvic fracture' part, that doesn't appeal. But, crikey, I love watching it. You give me some old weather-girl in an asymmetric off-the-shoulder bit of tangerine froth, twirling gamely with a cheery but somehow panic-stricken grin, and I'm glued.

So, being asked if I wanted to go to places named after Queen Victoria seemed quite a spiffy proposition. There seemed to be no hidden 'You have to adopt a child in each country' or 'You're taking a Special Needs Recorder Ensemble with you, travelling by tricycle' agenda at work, so instead of scrawling a big "NO!" on the paper and faxing it back to my agent, I said we should talk about it.

When the nice lady told me the locations of all the places that were named after Queen Victoria I was very excited. They were all over the shop – Antarctica, Canada, Hong Kong. There was even a Victoria Coach Station right here in our own capital!

Then we went from the kind of lunch meeting where you all get very enthusiastic and spit bits of breadstick over each other and go 'Wow, Antarctica, Victoria Coach Station!' to the kind of office meeting where you realise that going to places called Victoria isn't actually a television programme, it's a holiday.

So, a bit like apes rubbing sticks together and realising they might end up with jacket potatoes, we started to talk about why there were all these places called Victoria, and how come they were so widespread and had anybody minded all their nice place names in their own languages being hijacked by this one monicker (or monarcher).

And that led us to the Empire. That huge old elephant in the living room of our history. That time when the world was our cloakroom and, by golly, we were going to put our names on the pegs. And then the original idea swivelled around a bit: we would go to places called Victoria, and in doing that, we would try to tell a little bit of the story of the British Empire – this lumpy, unmanageable and, sometimes, almost unmentionable thing that had grown to its biggest by the end of Victoria's reign.

In 1897, Queen Victoria had been on the throne for sixty years, and during that time the British Empire had grown by more than ten times its former size. It covered a fifth of the earth's surface, and included a quarter of its population. By 1914 it controlled a quarter of the world's economy and had a population of more than 450 million people. It was the largest empire the world had ever known. It became popular to call it 'the Empire on which the sun never sets' – though I learnt later that a Sri Lankan politician once said, 'That's because God doesn't trust the British in the dark.'

I didn't know any of that when I started work on the programme. In fact, I had only the vaguest idea what the British Empire was. I had in my mind images culled from Somerset Maugham and Edgar Wallace. One book of his, *Sanders of the River* I believe it was called, left a very strong impression in my mind that only an Englishman could rule over 'natives' and make them see sense, so that was somehow our job; not always pleasant, and seeming in this case to involve being paddled upriver in a dugout canoe to dispense justice in the jungle, but it was a duty that had to be done.

Other reading, Agatha Christie in particular, fostered an idea of the Colonial man – someone who had made his fortune in some part of Empire, as a rubber-planter in Malaysia possibly, or in tea or coffee – as a good sort, often blue-eyed, usually weatherbeaten, and not usually the murderer. He was quite often to be found smashing a teak-hard fist into the jaw of a foreigner, a cad or an aesthete.

So as a child, and a voracious reader, I knew that all over the world men in starched and wilting dress shirts, or jodhpurs, and bitter disillusioned chain-smoking ladies in tea dresses, whose sexual allure had faded in the fierce heat of the sun, were living out their lives on verandas, in bungalows and 'whites only' tennis clubs to a soundtrack of chirping insects and the whir of ceiling fans, and that they were all something to do with the British Empire.

In the 1950s I lived in a white world. I had a book called *Children of Many Lands*. We lived in England, and everyone else lived in Many Lands. And we were the lucky ones. We spoke English, which was the top language, and we weren't foreign.

I knew there was something called the British Empire, which was something good, a Good Thing, but also made one a little bit uncomfortable, because it seemed to be to do with God and church and the Brownies and being decent. As a child I could never get on with God; the thought of him always brought up a whole slew of guilt and unease, and a conviction that I was a bad, bad person and one day he was going to tell me so.

Brownies gave me some of the same feelings, with the added worry of tying the tie. The Brownie tie then – I don't know what they have now, a pashmina probably – was a baffling back-to-front affair that could only be fastened by reciting a mumbled mantra that went something like 'Left over right, right over left'. Or possibly the other way round. When my son joined the Cubs, I was delighted to find this kind of sartorial battiness was still up and running, as his neckerchief, to get the sharp points necessary for true Cub preparedness, had to be held between the teeth while it was twisted, and then whacked on the banisters.

So yes, the Empire was bunged into that folder in my childish mental filing cabinet. It was hot, worthy and we were definitely in charge. I tried to think what I had been taught at school. Certainly that Great Britain was pink on the atlas, and that there were lots of other pink countries, and they belonged to us. No explanation was proffered that I recall – it was just a given. We owned all these other places, and we could go there whenever we wanted, a bit like having a static caravan at Filey. We could go there when we fancied doing a bit of sheep-shearing or rubber-planting, but I can't remember any mention of them coming here.

England was the hub of the world, in my mind, and lucky us, all over the globe lots of happy, laughing natives were chopping down bananas, picking tea, wrapping lumps of butter and sending it all our way, like so many benevolent country relatives, wanting nothing more than to be part of our great Empire family. These people were all 'natives': they were Natives of Many Lands and, like the dolls in national dress that so many of us collected in those dull days before recreational drugs, they could only really have one costume or prop per country – a turban, a fur parka, a machete.

These were my memories, as I came to gather my thoughts at the start of this television project, but I wanted to check I wasn't wildly off the mark. I didn't want to totally misrepresent my education. I went to a second-hand-book shop, and was thrilled to spot two junior-school textbooks, Johnstons *New Picture Geographies* Books One and Three, published in 1948 and 1950 respectively. It's quite likely that very similar books were being hoicked out of the geography cupboard at my own school, Fairfield County Primary in 1960, when I was seven.

Book One – *Peoples of the World*, by C. Midgeley. With C. Midgeley you get no namby-pamby let's-try-to-see-both-sides-of-the-question nonsense. He tells it like it is. This is Midgeley on the vexed question of the robbing of Aboriginal land in Australia by the British. I quote: 'Captain Cook found a part of Australia that was not desert. He said this was such a lovely land that Britain should look after it.' Can't argue with that, Midge.

I knew our programme, which is basically a travelogue, a fridge-magnetty whiz round the Empire, could never give more than a fleeting insight into the complicated and sensitive issues of race, subjugation, and exploitation that have to accompany any look at this subject – and we all worried that we would say the wrong thing, through ignorance or making inadvertently arrogant assumptions. In Midgeley's world, however, there is a clear line - no need for any wishy-washy hand-wringing. Issues are faced up to, and dealt with. Let me quote him on slavery:

In the old days of slavery, much harm was done to the poor natives. Now, however, slavery is finished; and in such countries as the West Indies, British West Africa and Malaya, the coloured peoples are glad to belong to the British Empire.

And where we would perhaps hesitate even to try and sum up an entire nation, Midgeley can knock off a race per paragraph:

> There are many different peoples in India. In the north are brave big men, who once did not like us, but are now our friends. In some other parts of the country the people are smaller. They have not red skins, like the Indians of North America. They are not black, like the negroes of Africa. They are brown in colour. Most of them are called Hindus.

So there we are – in the north, big and friendly like Cyril Smith; everywhere else, smaller. That's India.

Midgeley's books confirmed my childhood sense that the Empire was no more than a very large out-of-town hypermarket. He describes our 1950s breakfast table – our Canadian bread spread with New Zealand butter, or margarine made with oils from the Gold Coast, our Indian tea, or our Kenyan coffee sweetened with West Indian sugar. He says,

> In all parts of the world men and women have been at work growing the food which you have eaten. Hot lands and cool lands, forest lands and grass lands, have sent you their crops. English-speaking people thousands of miles away, black people, brown people and yellow people, have all done their share.

How marvellous, not only sending us a full English breakfast but in our own language. I felt the least I could do was go round the world and say thank you.

1

Ghana

We never stayed more than a day or two in each country. I had said right from the outset that I could only do the programme at all if each block of filming was completed within fourteen days, including travel to and from home. This was because I didn't want to leave my children for longer than that, but it did overlie every trip with a terrible *Challenge Anneka* sense of panic, of time being short – sometimes I felt we were like the documentary equivalent of the Keystone Kops, screeching to a halt in a country, spilling out of our bus, filming, chucking all the gear back to the boot and driving off at top speed, waving our footage like so many truncheons. So, I can't claim the whole thing to be much more than a better-produced, much lovelier-looking version of the talks with slides beloved of the Women's Institute.

The first trip, in March, was to Ghana, Jamaica and Newfoundland – Ghana and Jamaica to tell the story of the British Slave trade, and Newfoundland as the first British colony and the site of the first transatlantic cable station.

I flew to Accra in Ghana one Friday – shattered from just finishing a draft of a television drama I was working on, *Housewife, 49*, and for once looking forward to a flight as an opportunity to have a nice lie-down with no laundry to do. We landed around ten p.m. – and there was that usual discombobulating feeling of any strange airport at night. I haven't done a huge amount of travelling, but I've been to Ethiopia and Zimbabwe, so it didn't feel totally unknown.

1

During the two-hour drive to the hotel, one of our crew, Holly, who'd come to meet us, said the service at the hotel could be a bit slow, and perhaps we should order food now so it would be ready when we got there. Then followed a very convoluted conversation on the driver's mobile, about sandwiches and vegetarians. I'm a vegetarian, but sometimes it makes life so complicated I feel like giving it up and living on veal. However, it was all hands to the pump sandwich-wise at the hotel – we had the impression that the minute we pulled up at Reception they'd be running out with baps.

We arrived and checked in. I was starting to get a bit boiled round the eyes and my contact lenses felt like Formica. Holly asked the receptionist where the sandwiches would be. She looked like we'd asked her where Michael Flatley kept his spare tap shoes. She made a very slow call to the kitchen. Then she reluctantly imparted the information that the sandwiches had been made and could be had in the restaurant. Hoopla.

It was a very dimly lit hotel, a lot of brown going on, tiled walkways and closed shops. I just wanted to eat and go to bed. We finally tracked down the restaurant, and the sight we're so used to in English eateries in small towns at 23.01 – all the chairs on the tables and the staff sitting down in their shirt-sleeves faffing about with receipts. Mention of sandwiches met with blank looks all round. Holly said could they perhaps make some. The main receipt-faffer pulled a 'might, might not' sort of face. He headed off for the kitchen. It was like waiting for someone to bring you the other blue ones in a size seven. I gave up and went to my room.

Some time later I was asleep when a knock on my door turned out to be a waiter proffering a huge plate of very tiny cold chips and some coleslaw. I took it, not because I wanted it but because I couldn't be sure it wasn't breakfast.

~ *Introduction* ~

For more than three hundred years West Africa was the prime source of slaves brought to the New World in European ships, mainly Portuguese and British. During that period perhaps 10 million Africans were sold as slaves by the coastal African chiefs. Moved by humanitarian indignation, Britain ended her own participation in the slave trade in 1807, and abolished slavery in the 1830s. Reluctantly, the British government was obliged to take some responsibility for its former small and scattered African settlements. Defending them against the expanding Asante empire led first to a protectorate, then to the colony of the Gold Coast, which became independent as the Republic of Ghana in 1957.

Ghana's history since independence has been one of coups, corruption, and military dictatorships. Once one of Africa's richest countries, it fell into a catastrophic decline, which was only reversed thirty years later.

As we drove north from Accra into central Ghana, the temperature rose until it reached a baking, humid 42–3 degrees celsius. The blue of the sky was hidden behind a shimmering grey heat haze. There were roadworks everywhere – the country's infrastructure was under renovation – but as the Tarmac was laid, dust floated up into the thick blanket of heat. The roads were lined with vast areas of scrub interspersed with rows of banana trees. We couldn't see any farmhouses, and it was tempting to help ourselves to what looked like wild fruit, but we were warned not to. 'The man will see you,' our driver assured us. 'He will know you're doing it. He's there somewhere.'

Between the villages that had grown up at points on either side of the road, there were many little stalls, made from four poles supporting a palm-frond roof, that shaded a bench where goods were displayed for sale: a few vegetables, two or three eggs, the occasional alarmingly large rat and what looked like prairie dogs, boned and dried flat; huge snails slimed over one another in blue plastic bowls, and tatty polythene bags were filled with drinking water. By the roadside, clusters of oil-palm fruit sweltered in the heat.

Suddenly we would find ourselves in a largish village or town teeming with people who went about their lives out of doors. Women in loose, colourful dresses brightened up the dusty paths, and children played, or swept the approach to their small mud-walled houses. There seemed always to be a coffin or two under construction, and a surprising number of taxis. In one small town there must have been forty or fifty parked in the sunshine, waiting for business, their yellows, reds, blues and greens making a vivid splash.

Eventually we arrived at our destination: Assin Manso. This was where the story of the slave trade began. On the long, arduous journey south to the coast, chained tribespeople would be sorted here by age and sex, and sold into slavery. Then, after a brutal march of hundreds of kilometres, a wash in the muddy waters of Donkor Nsuo, or Slave River, would transform them into a more presentable and desirable acquisition to the waiting slave trader.

∼ Human Gold ∼

For many centuries a thriving trade had brought captives from the African interior across the Sahara through such great cities as Timbuktu to the Mediterranean slave markets. A distinguished visitor to Fez was given fifty male and fifty female slaves, ten eunuchs, twelve camels, one giraffe and twenty civet cats. Each cat was worth ten times more than a male slave.

Fanciful pictures of real horrors stimulated European indignation

When Portuguese merchants began to nose round the West African coast, they represented an attractive new market for the slave traders. At first they were not enthusiastic: they had come for gold or ivory, and a perishable human cargo was more troublesome, but it filled any spaces in the hold. Slaves were barely profitable because there was only a limited home demand: they could be used as singers, dancers and domestic servants, but were often paraded as little more than a fashion accessory.

Kidnapping the natives reduced costs, but this practice was abandoned once a recognised protocol evolved. Permission to trade was sought from a local ruler, who would share in the profits; some modest accommodation would be erected on the coast – the first was built in 1443 – to include a warehouse for the slaves. Prices varied according to the market: a brisk war brought a sharp reduction, while a period of peace sent them high; horses, which in early days were worth up to 15 slaves, were exchanged for no more than 5 or 6 a piece as the supply increased.

For more than a century Portugal had the field almost to itself. Then, in June 1494, Pope Alexander VI divided the – as yet – undiscovered globe between Spain and Portugal. The Spanish would have the Americas minus Brazil, and Portugal would take the rest. The new Protestant nations would later object, but Spain held on to the southern parts of America. Portugal lost most of its eastern empire to the Dutch and British, who arranged to divide it between them, broadly along the Equator: England would concentrate on India, the Dutch on the Indonesian archipelago. And all of the northern European nations intruded into West Africa.

The demand for slaves exploded with the discovery of the New World. Over the next three hundred years as many as ten million Africans were uprooted and transported across the Atlantic.

British slaving along the Gold Coast developed in the

1660s; the new West Indian colonies needed slaves to work the sugar plantations. The Royal African Company, with the Duke of York as chairman, followed the usual British method, of turfing out other Europeans, beginning with the seizure of Cape Coast Castle (Cabo Corso) in 1664.

Outside Assin Manso, close to the river, there is a modest visitors' centre where we met Adjekulai Alensah, a young man in charge of the area, who was well versed in the horrors of the past. 'Some European writers claimed that, because our ancestors couldn't read or write, some of the allegations made about how marketplaces were organised in the Western empires can't be proved. But we have a way of preserving our history. Some events were documented by the Arabs who traded with our ancestors, and others in our ancestors' ritual, drama, dancing and folklore, which has come down to us.'

He described the thousands of almost-naked captives, 'men, women and children over ten years old', who were shackled, chained and marched barefoot, from the largest slave market in the country at Salaga, through the rainforest to Assin Manso. Some had been snatched from their villages; others were prisoners-of-war, debtors or criminals. 'As they walked, those who couldn't continue were tied to trees to be eaten by wild animals or were shot. No one could fake sickness in the hope that they'd be set free. If you wanted to survive, you continued the walk.' All of them were at the mercy of the leader of the caravan and could be made to walk for days without rest, with just enough food to survive. 'Sometimes they bought people along the way, or a powerful leader would over-power or kill another leader and take over his caravan. The slaves arrived at Assin Manso exhausted and half-starved. Many tried to escape and were killed. Women were raped. Those who survived were brought to the river where they were made to eat fat to recover their energy, and washed.'

Many stories are told about the lengths to which the leaders went in the interests of a good sale. 'After washing the slaves, they removed the chains from their legs and made them jump to prove their strength. Also, they would open their mouths to find out their age from their teeth. In those days they found it hard to detect the age of an African. When you are a teenager your jaw or teeth won't be like those of an adult. If you are older, the colour of your teeth is different.' None of them knew what was going to happen. All they knew for certain was that they had been forcibly taken from their homes and marched to the coast. 'The local people thought the Europeans in their castles were eating our ancestors because those who were marched to the coast never returned. Many people tried to escape so many killings took place here. Some local people didn't like what was going on but they were in a minority and could do nothing.'

Adjekulai led us from the centre through an open blue gateway, each gate bearing a picture of a slave in broken chains, then under an archway with a notice that read, 'Welcome to the slave river.' 'The painting demonstrates the kind of treatment our ancestors received,' he explained. 'The broken chain shows that we have broken our chains and are free for ever.' A rough, narrow track overhung by giant bamboo led through another arch, marked 'last bath,' to a small tributary. Large brilliantly patterned butterflies flew past us. Huge soldier ants had built a causeway across the path, then lined up on either side of it to guard the workers who were carrying dirt and grass along it. Apparently they can kill an elephant by climbing up its trunk and biting the inside, which drives them mad. If one bit us we'd know about it. If more than fifty bit us, we might end up dead.

It was very moving to sit under the bamboo on the wide steps that led to the muddy river and remember those terrified people. For Adjekulai, it was still a painful collective memory and he was glad that we were going to bring the truth about what had happened to TV. Nearby there was a tree stump to which some captives had been chained as they waited their turn to be washed. 'We have two rivers. In the rainy season the level of this one comes up to the last step so they washed them in the other river. They were never allowed to wash themselves,' he told us. 'The owners chained the captives to the trees, then washed them in batches without removing their chains.'

He went on to describe what happened next: 'After washing them, they took them to the main town where they tied them to trees until a dealer came to buy them, then took them to the coast to sell them to the merchants.'

Back at the visitors' centre, he showed us a series of simple, local paintings depicting the captives and their plight: being brought to Assin Manso; washing in the river; a European in a top hat buying female slaves; then two dealers assessing a row of men. There are pictures of slaves being beaten by white men, a slave being branded, and a picture of the infamous interior of a tightly packed slave ship bound for the Americas.

The nearby graveyard contained a number of un-adorned brick tombs for descendants of slaves who had wanted to return to their homeland, and a series of stone slabs on which were recorded the names of those who had considered Assin Manso to be their spiritual resting place. It was a stark reminder of the extent and longevity of the human suffering caused by the spread of empire and the consequent need for slaves.

Later, we headed into the village. Telegraph wires were strung wildly over shanty rooftops, and shop-keepers traded from inside darkened doorways. In the distance we could hear children singing and clapping. Every now and then a cheer went up. People sat quietly in the shade, until we tried to balance our camera on a small stone plinth. Immediately we were told that this was ill-advised: it was the village chief's speaking block. When we met his right-hand man we apologised and asked how we could compensate for the mistake. 'Gifts,' was the reply. We asked nervously what he had in mind. It turned out that fifty dollars (about twenty-seven pounds) and two cans of Fanta would do the trick. We handed them over and got on with filming.

At the top of the hill, we found a glorious colonial house that once had been the property of the local slave-master. The three trees standing near it had once been used as tethering posts for recalcitrant slaves. It was shocking to hear that such inhumanity had taken place so close to the house, and we wondered why the trees had not been cut down given what they represented. We felt uncomfortable: there had been nothing inevitable about what had happened here. The horror had been caused by greed and calculation.

From Assin Manso, the slaves were marched a further forty-five kilometres to the coast. There, they were taken to one of the thirty-two castles or forts the Europeans had built along Ghana's coastline to await embarkation for the New World. Initially gold and timber had been traded at the forts for guns, and they were used as headquarters by marauding Europeans who wanted to penetrate the Ghanaian interior, but all Westerners struggled to survive in the hostile conditions.

∽ The Worst Journey in the World ∽

The slaves' tragedy started with the trek to the coast, on which they were chained together in lines or 'coffles', used as pack animals until they were confined in the coastal slave quarters or 'barracoons'. At the coast they were briskly sorted by the ships' surgeons into 'sound' and 'Mackrons' – ill or old. The sound were then smeared with palm oil and branded: DY, for Duke of York, or RAC, for Royal African Company, before they were sent on the 'middle passage', to the Caribbean or, increasingly, to the British North American colonies. Although the ships' commanders were anxious to land as many healthy slaves as possible in the New World, the tension, fear and – sometimes – guilt inclined even the humane to habitual brutality, while sadistic crews made the journey almost insufferable. Many died of starvation, disease, ill-treatment and desperation. The crews suffered too: their pay was miserable, and mortality was higher even than it was among the slaves.

*The slave's tragedy started with the trip to the coast,
chained and used as pack animals*

∾ White Man's Graveyard ∾

The west coast of Africa became known as 'the white man's graveyard', and it was usual to keep a supply of coffins on hand because a new arrival might die within twenty-four hours of disembarkation. More than two years' residence was reckoned a mortal risk. When the Portuguese attempted to colonise, they sent the nation's undesirables, who included condemned criminals. Spain sent two thousand young Jews, all of whom died quickly. A more common solution to early death was to intermarry with the locals, producing hardier mixed-race families of 'caboceers' who acted as intermediaries with local magnates.

Our journey took us to Cape Coast Castle, which in 1664 had become the centre of British operations in Ghana when a group of soldiers had taken the original, much smaller, building from the Dutch. Now a World Heritage Site, Cape Coast Castle is a splendid colonial fort built on rocks overlooking the Atlantic. Ironically, given its history, it is a beautiful place, with thick, sun-bleached walls towering over a vast cobbled square. Extensively rebuilt by the British in 1768, the southern part of the building was replaced with a large fortified battery mounted with cannons that still point out to sea, pyramids of cannonballs beside them.

After a few minutes filming beneath the searing sun in the central square where the slaves would have been auctioned, we were feeling the effects even though we were wearing hats and sunblock, and had bottles of water. It must have been so much worse for those who were bought and sold with no one catering for their most basic needs.

At one end of the square, just below the Victorian church, a tunnel leads down a steep slope into almost complete darkness. Here, men and women were segregated in separate cells. As many as a thousand male and five hundred female slaves were crammed into the maze of tiny dungeons at a time, huddled together so that they could barely move. A tunnel cuts through the floor of each for the disposal of human waste. In fact, the floors would have been slick with it, contaminating the food that was thrown in by the guards through a tiny hole in an end wall. A shaft of daylight, almost blinding in its intensity, shone through into the darkness. The only sound that the exhausted, terrified and malnourished slaves would have heard was the relentless crashing of the waves on the beach outside.

The slaves' fear of the unknown and the conditions in which they were kept made many so violent that they were under constant watch. The most troublesome were flogged and put into the condemned cell where it was even hotter and darker than it was in the others. Once there, they were often forgotten and left to die.

The slaves endured this regime for days, weeks or months, depending on when the next ship was due. Eventually, when it arrived, they were herded through the Door of No Return and boarded. We were told that many lives were lost on the voyage because the slaves' accommodation was so cramped and illness was rife. The traders appeared to consider them worthless.

Today, in the shade of the castle walls just outside the Door of No Return, fishermen sit beneath patchwork awnings mending their nets, their long wooden boats pulled up beside them. Further along the white-sand beach, children dash in and out of the waves or play football. It's a far cry from what happened here all those years ago.

~ Amazing Grace! ~

John Newton, a slave captain, but later a clergyman and author of 'Amazing Grace', 'Glorious Things of Thee Are Spoken' and 'How Sweet the Name of Jesus Sounds' had once been held captive by an African slave owner, 'the villainous Mrs Chow'. During his slaving career, he does not seem to have been much concerned with the morality of the trade: he avoided unnecessary cruelty, but was unconcerned about the fate of a woman he refused to buy because she had 'long breasts'.

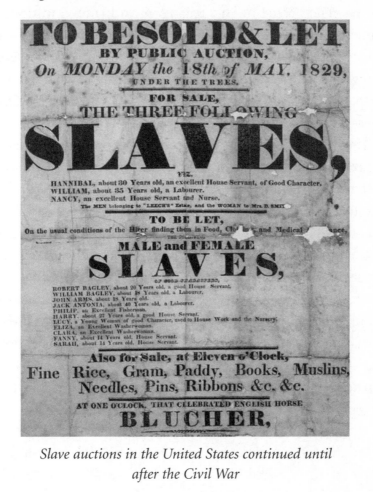

Slave auctions in the United States continued until after the Civil War

∼ A Wonderfully Profitable Trade ∼

Slave ships began their voyage laden with freight – Birmingham arms and metal goods, or Manchester cotton fabrics. African tribal rulers made a comfortable income from acting as middlemen: they took a profit from the slaves and the trade goods. With the help of British muskets the Asante empire became the dominant force of the Gold Coast. The West Indian sugar planters made vast fortunes, with slave labour, and the final returns on the sale of rum, sugar and other Caribbean products showed an impressive gain for the investors who had initially funded the slave ships and their cargoes. In Glasgow, Whitehaven, Liverpool and Bristol, family fortunes were built on the slave trade, and the participants – such as the Barretts, later of Wimpole Street – became respectable and prosperous.

Some mixed-race dynasties did well for themselves on the Gold Coast. The Corkers (Caulkers or Crackers) were led by the famous Senhora Doll, 'Duchess of Sherbro', who kept a permanent army to control and protect the hundreds of slaves she held awaiting sale. Some rebelled: six Asante enslaved by the Dutch killed themselves 'in a savage and inhuman manner, cut their throats, and when they did not succeed the first time, they repeated the thrusts 3 or 4 times . . . The yard of the noble company's chief castle was thus turned into a blood bath.'

We had followed the slavers' route so far, but now we wanted to see the Ghana of today and discover what legacy, if any, of the Empire had been left. From the castle we travelled to Cape Coast itself, a large sprawling town that has been built up round its original colonial centre. At first glance, the majority of the people and the buildings seem poor, but in fact many businesses service a thriving community, with a spiritual awareness that was reflected in the names of some shops we passed, such as the Lord is My Shepherd Tyres and Save Our Souls Electrics.

Victoria Park was among our first stops. The name conjured up visions of boating-lakes, daffodils, sycamores and manicured lawns, but we found ourselves in a large open space with plastic bags strewn everywhere. At one end, just yards from the pristine turquoise sea, a wooden boat was for sale, beside stinking piles of debris where pigs foraged under clouds of mosquitoes. There was an overwhelming stench of sewage and rotting rubbish. Between this area and a flight of huge stone steps forty or fifty yards away, there was a dusty football pitch, complete with a concrete stand and a forbidding bust of Queen Victoria. The latter had been installed when the British Empire still held sway. That day we found sixty passionate young footballers, aged between seven and seventeen, in frenzied pursuit of a ball, inspired by Ghana having qualified for the World Cup.

The boys were being coached by the charismatic Kofi Amuah, who was happy to talk to us and passionate about what he was doing. 'I've been a coach since 1996,' he told us. 'I realised I have the potential to teach kids, and that the way I can get through to them is through sport. Apart from football, I'm trying to teach them discipline and give them education. Most of these boys are coming from the street. They have parents, or maybe only one parent, who are very poor but they take care of them. I visit the small football pitches where they play, talk to them and try to put them into schools. I talk to their parents or other relatives about the importance of education. Sometimes they give money to put them in school.' At other times Kofi dips into his savings to pay for uniform, shoes and books.

Among the children we watched that day, one wanted to be an architect, another a car mechanic. They all wore a smart football strip, donated by Kofi or other benefactors. 'They're so proud of the new kit that they have never lost a match while wearing it,' he told us.

Young Ghanaians are proud of their nationality, but many are aware of the poverty and deprivation in their lives because they are increasingly exposed to Western culture. Kofi was doing his best to help some transcend it.

We wanted to know how Ghanaians feel about their place in the world and decided that the person most likely to know would be a comedian: a sharp political view of events is a prerequisite of the job. We had arranged to meet Fritz Baffour, a comedian with his own TV chat show, for supper at one of the smartest restaurants in Cape Coast. It turned out to be quite different from the restaurant we had visited previously, in the centre of town. Two large women had sat behind a table with three enormous bowls of sauce. A sheep's skull floated on the surface of one, with a couple of jawbones. Each customer was given a plastic bowl that contained a sizeable dumpling, which they took to the women who poured over it a generous quantity of sauce.

When we arrived to meet Fritz, we were invited into the small kitchen, to watch the meal being prepared. First, two girls sitting on three-legged stools washed and chopped the ingredients. Then they made a sticky okra gumbo to dip dumplings, plantain, red peas and a piece of fish. It was all cooked quickly on a tiny coal-fired stove pot.

The evening was close and humid, and so we sat outside

at a table under a canopy. Fritz was a giant of a man, with an infectious chuckle. Over the meal, he explained the common Ghanaian perception of Britain: 'We have a relationship that can never be broken. We were under British colonial rule and most of our infrastructure and state institutions originate from the British colonial system. We still send a lot of our people to Britain for training. Informally, though, most Ghanaians look to the States. It's less like visiting your old headmaster!'

He was illuminating when he spoke of slavery. There had been, he said, a fundamental difference between the Arab and the European trades: 'The Arab trade was very much part of the Arab cultural infrastructure where slaves were more like servants and given the chance to rise and become a general, the head of a harem, a eunuch or a prime minister. European chattel slavery, on the other hand, was direct ownership where slaves were property and had no rights whatsoever.' He believed that the unprecedented scale of the transatlantic slave trade had led to an irretrievable breakdown in the country's social structures because greed had taken over and soon no one could be trusted: 'People sold their brothers and sisters, their friends. Then they started raiding weaker tribes and villages so they could trade the people for guns and so on. It was a very bad period for Africa. Although today people here don't think about the slave trade *per se*, the man walking down the street has been affected by the fact that our social structures were broken down . . . We're getting out of our dark age now and are realising that things like the tenets of democracy – integrity, justice, accountability, human rights, women's rights and so on – are very important.'

Ghana finally became independent in 1957. What had happened when the British left the country, we wondered. 'They left people who could run the show and be inclined towards Britain,' Fritz told us. 'But that didn't happen because we had a very far-sighted leader in Kwame Nkrumah, who had visited Britain and spent time in America.' Nkrumah wanted Ghana to be a classless society, on the American model, and made far-reaching changes as he attempted to lift his country out of poverty. 'But a certain class structure that the British left existed within the army – officers and men – which often intervened in our democratic process. Some people believe that's what took us backwards. Eventually, it dawned on us all that we had to have a disciplined army. Now the Ghanaian Army is seen as one of the best peace-keeping forces in the world.'

As we had driven through Cape Coast, poverty had been all too apparent. 'We are poor materially,' Fritz said, 'and poverty can be a killer because it stifles innovation and motivation, and is leading to a situation where we believe in handouts. There's a lot of work to do but there's hope, too, because we have a vibrant transcultural younger generation coming back. I'm not saying they'll be the saviours but at least they'll be able to explain how systems work in Europe from the African point of view. So, I see Africa blooming.'

Although some Ghanaians head for Europe where 'we believe advancement and enlightenment comes from' to escape the poverty, Fritz has no intention of following them: 'I look to Britain. If somebody stops me by virtue of my colour, I'd rather stay here and go through the pain.

And if I triumph then I triumph with my people. That's what's important.'

We had one last appointment on our whistle-stop schedule, with Nana and Imahkus Ofoku, who were originally from New York. Nana, now elderly but looking astonishingly youthful, thanks in part to his dreadlocks, worked for the New York City Fire Department, while Imahkus was a human-resources administrator. They had returned to their roots in Africa and settled in Ghana, where they have established One World, a 'half-way house' for others wanting to follow their example. Circular terracotta-coloured cabins with thatched roofs in well-cared-for gardens provide a welcome oasis from Ghana's apparent chaos.

Nana and Imahkus felt the need to reclaim their heritage: 'Our book of study tells us that we're going to be sent away from the land of our origin to a strange land, that we'll be captured and sold into slavery under the rulership of the people who are not even a nation and that they would treat us evil for four hundred years. We've been told that. And we are also told that, when we make certain changes in our minds and spirits, some of us will return to the land of our origin. To come home,' Nana said, 'I'm here looking for my inheritance and for my family. I'm looking for the area from which my ancestors were kidnapped and taken against their will to a foreign land. I think the ultimate reason for returning home is to unite as a people. To see how we can work together to better our conditions and to survive in this new economic age.'

While the couple were still living in New York, Imahkus had made a visit to the Cape Coast Castle dungeons.

It had been a life-changing experience: 'When I went into the women's dungeon, I heard voices. I could smell bodies. I heard people crying and moaning. And I felt a pain like you would not believe. I remember crying and crying and hearing these screams until I realised that some of them were mine. Then I got the comforting feeling that people were around me, touching me, assuring me that I was all right – "You're home now. It's OK." When I came out I looked around for the people, because I'd heard them and I could still smell them. I could feel their spirit so strong. I knew that I would never be the same person again. I also knew that I was going to live the rest of my life in Africa, an African person coming home.'

When she returned to New York, she suggested Nana came to visit. He, too, had an overwhelming sense of the spirits in the dungeons. 'You could smell the stench. You could feel the energy of the ancestors in there. I asked the guide if I could spend a little time on my own in there in the dark. That was a horrific experience.' But it persuaded him that Imahkus was right: they should leave New York.

Their move was not without problems. First, they had to leave their family in the States, but they have made a family home in Ghana where their six children 'always have a place to lay their head'. Then they had to adjust to the language and culture. Both fell ill. 'I remember being real sick one day', Imahkus told us, 'sweating and shivering and taking all these herbs. When I got to the doctor I was crawling on my hands and knees, I said, "I'm so sick, Doctor. I want to die." This doctor smiled at me. "Welcome to Ghana," he replied. "Welcome home." I thought, The man must be out of his mind. Welcome to

Ghana? He said, "You are not Ghanaian until you've had a bout of malaria." So now I have had it a few times, and we are seasoned Ghanaians.'

When Nana and Imahkus moved to Ghana, they lived without a flush toilet or electricity for two years. 'When we got the water running, we tied a red ribbon across the toilet door, had a ceremony of dancing and singing, then a traditional cutting of the ribbon. That was an exciting moment,' Nana said. 'Then they told me, "Nana, you have to get electricity." I said, "Why? I was born in New York City and I've seen more electricity than you'll see in your life." Living with candlelight and lanterns at night was so romantic. But eventually we had to get electricity for the sake of the computer and so on.'

Since they have been in Ghana, they have set up a commemorative ceremony, Through the Door of No Return, for 'brothers and sisters from the diaspora coming home for the first time to go into the castle dungeons and to be put into our ancestors' frame of mind as they travelled through that experience'. The aim is to honour those who were taken away by re-enacting what they endured. During the ceremony, Imahkus explains 'who and what Africa is. What our journey is', and there are songs about the slave experience. Afterwards, a local group of actors performs a play about the capture of slaves: 'villagers are going about their business when they are pounced on by foreigners, put in chains and shackles, then walked down into the castle dungeons while they're beaten'. The visitors are taken into the male and female dungeons, then the men cross the courtyard to meet the women at the Door of No Return. 'That is to let the ancestors know that we know of their fear and their confusion.' There is more singing, and everyone returns to the castle, to show the ancestors that 'We are home once more.' The couple hope that their work 'helps visiting African Americans to link up with their roots. There are some bonding spirits in these buildings and for some of these people it's a healing process. Our ancestors didn't know where they were going or whether they would ever go back to their village again and see their families. So we are also vessels that can help to release some of our ancestral spirits. It works both ways.'

Nana told us what had happened to the slaves when they reached their destination: 'To control a person you first have to break their spirit. It was done by renaming, by not allowing us to use our language or our traditional culture. It was a psychological process that was deliberate and brutal to separate the enslaved Africans from their land, family and culture. We're still fighting for equality.'

Despite missing Baskin-Robbins ice-cream, the American seasons and, of course, their friends and family, Nana and Imahkus are happy. They have fond memories of their lives in New York but 'We have never missed anyone or anything enough to want to give up the opportunity to live in our ancestral homeland.' A circle has been completed.

∾ Why did Christians No Longer Want to Buy Slaves? ∾

In 1799, the British public had become so indignant at the well-publicised evils of the slave trade that Lloyds of London stopped insuring slaves against 'natural death, ill treatment or . . . throwing overboard'. But not everyone was anti-slaving: the Liverpool MPs Banastre Tarleton, Isaac Gascoyne and Bamber Gascoyne forecast ruin for their city, which owed its prosperity to the trade. But the end was in sight. In 1807, the Slave Trade Abolition Act made any British participation a criminal offence.

Abolition of the trade – although slavery itself was still legal – baffled the Africans: 'Why do the Christians no longer want to buy slaves?' asked the Asante king. 'Is not their God the same as that of the Muslims, who continue to buy, kidnap and sell slaves just as they always have done?' The King of Bonny, further down the coast, declared that the trade must continue: 'That is the verdict of our oracle and the priests. They say that your country, however great, can never stop a trade ordained by God himself.'

Meanwhile, the caboceers and coastal chiefs, who faced an immediate reduction in their income, made the best of it. Such enterprising Euro-African merchants as Elizabeth Skelton, who named her new fort Victoria in 1825, and Mrs Bailey Lightburne, who sued the Navy unsuccessfully for destroying her barracoons, made use of the slaves by putting them to work in palm-oil production, used in soap-making and as a machine lubricant, acacia gum, hides, ivory and gold for export, and on foodstuffs for local consumption. Charles Heddle, another Euro-African trader, pioneered groundnut cultivation and was able to retire to a splendid French chateau.

∼ Victoria *Ends the Slave Trade* ∼

British attempts to persuade other nations to ban the trade were backed by the Royal Navy, which attempted to intercept slave ships. It was given a free hand to track down slavers by land and sea, to destroy slaving ports, wherever they might be, burning Spanish and Portuguese barracoons, usually having secured the agreement of the African rulers, and liberate the slaves.

It was a task that frigate crews relished: they had seen for themselves the horrors of the trade. The ships were not hard to find: the wind carried their stench for miles. If no slaves were found aboard, the presence of shackles or even extra planks, which might be used to build slave decks, was enough to warrant arrest. Generous bounties encouraged sailors to track them down, and by 1840 the Royal Navy had brought more than four hundred slave ships into Sierra Leone and released the captives. During the reign of George III the British had taken more than a million Africans to the New World. Now they were fighting slavery wherever they found it.

The slave trade in West Africa ended in 1851, with the bombardment of Lagos, a notorious slaving centre. The final shot in the action was not fired by a warship but by a rowing-boat that belonged to the British consul, tagging along behind the flotilla. Iron-built, she was capable of mounting rockets, and it was one such missile that exploded the fort's magazine. Her name was *Victoria*.

We left Ghana with a sense of relief. The heat and humidity had been overwhelming, and we all had upset stomachs. Our trip had been brief so we came away with a fleeting impression, but it was apparent to us all that the heart had been ripped out of Ghana. We were appalled by all that had happened there and Britain's part in it. For three hundred years, the people of Ghana had been told that their culture was worthless. Now, though, there are signs that the country is gearing up to meet the future.

∽ *The Aftershock* ∽

In 1834 British MPs voted to abolish slavery. However, the effect on African economies was catastrophic. Given time, coastal communities could adapt, but inlanders were faced with immediate problems; one African ruler found himself with eight hundred unemployable slaves on his hands and

The Asante capital, Kumasi, 'crowded with magnificence and novelty'

had most of them decapitated, eighty were spared – given to the executioner in payment for his services. For the slaves, liberty often meant little more than the freedom to starve: later, during Victoria's reign, one group complained that 'unless the *Queen* intended to give them something to eat they would prefer to serve their masters who supplied their wants'.

The Asante found the ending of slavery particularly difficult. Their empire, which had developed after the invasion of ancient goldfields in the seventeenth century, was rooted in great wealth, but it had been dependent on a constant supply of slaves. In 1819 a British visitor described his reception in the capital, Kumasi: 'An area of nearly a mile in circumference was crowded with magnificence and novelty . . . More than a hundred bands burst out at once on our arrival, with the peculiar airs of their several chiefs . . . At least a hundred large umbrellas, or canopies, which could shelter thirty persons, were sprung up and down by their bearers with brilliant effect, being made of scarlet, yellow and the most showy cloths and silks, and crowned on the top with crescents, pelicans, elephants, barrels, arms and swords of gold.' On top of that, the Asante commemorated any great event with human sacrifices, for which, of course, they needed slaves.

At first the British administration on the coast took pains not to meddle in the affairs of such powerful neighbours, and allowed slave traders to pass freely. But in 1841, when it assumed formal responsibility for scattered settlements, some regulation became inevitable, which meant war.

∽ Reluctant Imperialists ∽

Gradually political institutions of a European kind evolved in Gold Coast towns – among them the Fante Confederation, inspired by Dr James Africanus Horton, who began his career as an army surgeon and ended it as colonial magistrate and deputy governor. Its first constitution, agreed by the 'educated gentlemen' of the Gold Coast in November 1871, proposed a legislature with a king or president, a Great Seal (which was struck) and an executive charged with modernisation of the area. It was a striking demonstration of the speed with which Africans had adapted to European ideas and was far in advance of its time. Political power still rested with the traditional African chiefs, who saw these urban intellectuals as a threat to their own interests; British administration, still uncertain of its true role, greeted it with a distinct lack of warmth.

In 1868 young Fante succeeded in repelling an Asante invasion. Diplomats stepped in to smooth things over, but the Asante were aggrieved. In June 1873 an Asante army marched to the coast and attacked the British

Fante soldiers of General Wolseley's army

fort at Elmina; they were driven off but – unenthusiastical-ly, since the expense would be great – the British government decided on a punitive expedition, led by Sir Garnet Wolseley (immortalised by W. S. Gilbert as 'the very model of a modern major general'), to bring about a 'permanent peace'. Sir Garnet's West Indian, British, Haussa and Fante troops, equipped with mobile hospitals, bakeries and water-purifiers, occupied and destroyed Kumasi with the loss to themselves of only eighteen killed in action. Wolseley wrote to the Asante monarch: 'Your Majesty can no more prevent an army of white men marching into your territory . . . than you can stop the sun [from] rising.'

The Asante sued for peace but this presented the British government with a dilemma. The victory had been decisive but there was nothing to be gained from continuing their presence in West Africa. However, the British public thought otherwise. Delighting in the war correspondents' horrific reports – the *Illustrated London News*'s double-page spread of the hundreds of sacrificial victims in various stages of decomposition was especially satisfying – many lobbied for the imposition of 'civilisation'. Eventually, compromise was reached: the coastal states were grouped together as a colony, and an informal 'protectorate' extended some eighty miles inland to the southern borders of Asante territory.

Victorian governments were extremely reluctant to expand, or even to retain, African colonies. British jurisdiction of the coast was limited to the areas around the trading stations, and based on agreements with local chiefs. In 1865 a House of Commons Select Committee had recommended withdrawal from all coastal settlements, except perhaps Sierra Leone. The public weren't interested, and colonies

The London Illustrated News pictured hundreds of Asante victims

cost money. When French competition seemed to threaten British trade on the Niger coast British traders suggested that a protectorate was introduced which would be agreed with local magnates, would not involve a transfer of sovereignty, and would only cost about five thousand pounds a year. Even this was too much, and would have to be paid for by closing existing consulates in Hawaii – reluctant imperialism indeed.

∼ Scramble for Africa ∼

Wolseley's expedition of 1874 had demonstrated how easily a modern army could defeat a far greater African force, so other European powers followed suit in what became known as the 'Scramble for Africa'. British indifference, even hostility, to colonisation switched to enthusiasm under the Conservative governments that dominated politics for the twenty years after 1885. This was just too late to affect the result of the Berlin West Africa Conference earlier that year, which determined to a great extent the future boundaries of African states.

The British negotiators at the Conference had remained reluctant to accept more colonial responsibilities. Their main concern was still to ensure that traders were not locked out of any part of Africa by other European powers. The price of this was the agreement that vast areas (now represented by the countries of Mali, Niger and Chad) should be regarded as French – mostly desert, 'very light land', as the prime minister, Lord Salisbury, cynically remarked – and that King Leopold of Belgium should be allowed personal control of the huge area that is today the Democratic Republic of Congo. It was a decision that was to have tragic consequences for the country in the twentieth and twenty first centuries.

In West Africa the coast between Ghana and the Cameroons was acknowledged as a British sphere of influence. Expensive military intervention by governments was avoided by the traditional device, used nearly three hundred years before in India, of permitting a London-based commercial company to negotiate with local magnates, using their own forces to settle any disputes which might arise. This idea appealed to the Conservative Colonial Secretary, Joseph Chamberlain, who was himself a businessman. Thanks principally to the invention of the magazine rifle, which enabled disciplined troops to fight off superior numbers, British chartered companies carved out great swathes of African territory for themselves. Later they were taken over by an understaffed, poorly funded Colonial Service.

The 3rd Earl Grey, who guided British colonial strategy for much of the mid-nineteenth century, had made clear his policy for West Africa: 'The real interest is gradually to train the inhabitants . . . in the arts of civilisation and government until they shall grow into a nation capable of protecting themselves and of managing their own affairs . . . it is not desirable . . . that the duty of governing and protecting the inhabitants of Western Africa should be thrown upon this country longer than can be avoided.' Easier said than done, however, and it was to be a hundred years before Grey's objective was realised.

∽ An Imperial Casualty ∽

In the settled conditions of the Gold Coast there was one last, singularly pointless war. In 1895 another assault took place on Kumasi. Again, there were few casualties, but the Queen's son-in-law, Prince Henry of Battenberg, died of fever, a casualty of imperialism.

2

Jamaica

We couldn't fly direct from Ghana to Jamaica, we had to go back to Heathrow, hang about for four hours or so, then fly on to Montego Bay. Tiger Aspect, the production company, very kindly arranged for me to have a massage at one of those hotels near the M4. It was the worst massage I've ever had. One, it was painful – like being beaten up with wind chimes. Two, the massage lady talked non stop, whispering a load of old nonsense about blue skies and rainbows, all in a very strong Spanish accent, so not only was it irritating and pointless, I had to strain to catch the exact wording.

Now, I should, of course, have been able, in an adult and mature way, to ask her politely to stop talking and perhaps also refrain from REALLY HURTING but I didn't – I get very inhibited in these situations, and all I did was get TENSER and TENSER until I thought I was going to burst out of my towel like the Incredible Hulk and chuck her and her massage table out of the window.

So when the rest of the crew and I became ill with a bug we'd picked up in Ghana, I was claiming for ages I didn't have a bug at all, just a lousy massage. Anyway, we were all ill in varying degrees the whole time we were in Jamaica. We were fine if we didn't eat, but it's hard to do a day's work in the heat if you don't eat – so we'd chomp something down, and say gamely that we felt fine, we were on the mend, then some hours later there would be a flurry of anxious enquiries about the whereabouts of the nearest lawies – well, you can imagine, it happens to everybody, and I wasn't the worst, and I didn't have to hold a camera on my shoulder in the boiling heat of Kingston.

It was cooler up in the Blue Mountains, in the rainforest. I knew we'd come to talk to the leader of the Maroons, the community of Jamaicans descended from the escaped slaves, the African Bushmen who waged a guerrilla war against the British and couldn't be defeated. We walked up a steep hill on our way to see the Kindah tree, under which the treaty with the British was signed, giving the Maroons freedom and autonomy. There was a wonderfully strong smell of marijuana, and I was quite cheered when I saw a bottle of white rum – it seemed just the ticket to put me right, but it was part of the Kindah ceremony and we had to wash our faces in it. (Because I'm worth it.)

It felt odd to be walking up the hill with all these people I'd never met. No one spoke to me, and I certainly wasn't going to strike up with the small-talk, but they all seemed very relaxed with the situation. We set up our camera to film the traditional dance the Maroon ladies do to celebrate the signing of the treaty, and the ladies, none in the first flush of youth, filmed the setting-up on the mobiles they had attached to their skirt waistbands. By the time our camera was on its tripod we were already on YouTube.

∽ *Introduction* ∽

In 1655, the British captured the Spanish Caribbean island of Santiago and renamed it Jamaica. After a halting start, when the island was a centre for buccaneers, the British invested in sugar plantations, imported African slaves to work them and amassed great fortunes for themselves, at the same time ensuring Jamaica's prosperity. Only in the nineteenth century did Baptist missionaries begin to educate the non-white population, who formed the majority of the island's people. Planter resistance led to violent revolts, the last of which, in 1865, caused the British government to abolish Jamaica's independent government and take over the island as a Crown Colony. In 1958 Jamaica joined the West Indian Federation, then left it in 1962 to become an independent nation.

Rather smaller than Northern Ireland and with a population of more than two-and-a-half million, Jamaica is the poorest island in the British West Indies. It has one of the world's highest murder rates and remains a centre of the drug trade, although it has recently inaugurated reforms.

Port Royal, near our first stop, Kingston, was once the capital of Jamaica and renowned as the richest and wickedest city in the world. During the seventeenth century it was a major trading and naval port, as well as a haven for pirates, most notably the infamous Welshman Henry Morgan, and Black Beard. They were a wild bunch who would return from raiding, laden with treasure, to celebrate in drinking and gambling dens, and brothels.

Of the old Port Royal all that remains is Fort Charles, a red-brick ruin on a spot of land a short journey from Kingston. It is reasonably well preserved, especially the charming living quarters, which are surrounded by trees. James Roberts, a historian at the University of the West Indies, joined us to paint a picture of Port Royal's boom-town days: 'Jamaica was the Sodom of the universe. The governors here were on a very long, loose piece of string so they could get up to mischief for a long time before the royal letter came. Port Royal was where the sailors spent their money. They wanted booze and this place had rum. In those days they used lead pipes to distil it so there was plenty of lead poisoning. Then there were the houses of ill-fame as well as a fair amount of theft. A lot of sailors ashore had had a boring voyage. They'd be wearing spiffy clothes in bad condition, they'd smell and they were ferocious. They never admitted to being pirates, though. In town they all claimed to be loyal, upstanding sea captains or privateers. There was probably a number of ex-slaves among them, indentured labourers and runaway ships' crew, as well as French- or Dutchmen and anyone else who wanted a job.

'The aim of many Englishmen was to come here, make a fortune, take it home and find themselves several notches up the social ladder. Henry Morgan was the classic example. He came out to Barbados as an indentured labourer yet became a successful privateer. He was tough, lucky and smart. He kept some of the loot and turned it into land.'

～ *Honest Fellows* ～

The colony of Jamaica had a difficult beginning. With a garrison of only a thousand soldiers, who were badly fed and equipped, the colony's survival depended on an anarchic collection of buccaneers. Cruel, ruthless and recklessly brave, the buccaneers were perhaps the most formidable irregular force ever assembled. They were recruited by Sir Thomas Modyford, governor of the island between 1664 and 1671, who described them as 'honest fellows, though occasionally too convivial', to harass the Dutch and Spanish throughout the Caribbean. Their most famous commander, Henry Morgan (c. 1635–88), shared the loot with his men but also with King Charles II, the Duke of York and Modyford; it was a profitable enterprise for all concerned. Knighted by the King and appointed lieutenant governor of Jamaica, Morgan became history's most respectable pirate.

Captain Sir Henry Morgan, buccaneer and governor

Port Royal's new-found stability did not last long: in 1692 an earthquake and a series of tidal waves swept most of the city and its inhabitants into the sea. It was divine retribution, some claimed. The British attempted to rebuild the town but fire and regular hurricanes made it so difficult that the government abandoned Port Royal for mainland Jamaica where they established the town of Kingston, which, during the eighteenth century, took over as a base for naval, merchant and fishing fleets, and has been the capital of the island ever since.

The remains of Fort Charles, originally one of six forts that protected Port Royal, stand at the tip of a twelve-mile-long peninsula that juts out into the sea opposite Kingston. Today it is so quiet that it is hard to imagine that it was the hub of seventeenth-century debauchery. We sat on the ramparts with James, who explained why Jamaica had been such a prize: first, it pirated wealthy Spanish galleons, but second, and more importantly, it produced the crop that the British craved: sugar. 'They started with cocoa and tried crops like cotton and indigo, but sugar was the one that made the big bucks. A blight hit cocoa, cotton didn't pay and indigo was too difficult. If indigo goes wrong, you end up with a pile of compost, but sugar could always be re-refined. Sugar is complicated but pretty resilient.' The British people were then unused to sweetened food, and sugar was deemed the height of luxury. Also, 'It paid well, it's shippable and it's addictive. English catering had been moving towards heavily sugared food from the 1590s when Drake and the like had been raiding sugar ships from Brazil. The West Indies fed this sweet tooth.'

∾ Sugar and Slavery ∾

The Jamaican sugar planters, perhaps eight hundred of them in all, controlled the government and ran Jamaica as they pleased. All became rich, and some very rich indeed.

Peter Beckford, who arrived in 1662 and died in 1720, made £1.5 million pounds in bank stock, a prodigious sum in those days (only ten families in England were believed to have incomes of more than £20,000). Beckford owned eight sugar estates, and at least two thousand slaves. His great-great-grandson William, author of the novel *Vathek*, was the richest man in England, with an income of £100,000, most of which he spent on the Gothic palace of Fonthill in Wiltshire, complete with a three-hundred-foot tower.

Men and women shared the hard labour of cutting sugar cane

From Fort Charles we went on to Kingston, where we were to meet Freddie McGregor, a Jamaican reggae star who lives in the foothills of the Blue Mountains. Along breezy

Ocean Boulevard, we passed Negro Aroused, a sculpture of a crouching man breaking free of his chains, then went into the grid of streets that make up the city's historic centre. Although many buildings were flattened during an earthquake in 1907, a number of elegant colonial structures remain, particularly along King Street where columned balconies jut out New Orleans-style over the street. Jamaica is a deeply religious country so the centre of the city was relatively quiet when we arrived on a Sunday. Many people were sleeping on the streets – homelessness is a serious problem – and Kingston is a dangerous city, especially in the centre. We became all too aware of this when our driver took a wrong turning and told us to duck out of sight.

As we drove up into the hills above Kingston, where Freddie lives, we were constantly aware of a heavy bass beat, which thumped out of almost every open door or window – more dub than reggae – and the scent of weed wafted on the breeze. We hoped Freddie would be able to tell us why the tiny island of Jamaica had been the birthplace of a sound that had spread across the world.

When we reached his modern, gated house, we were taken to his recording studio. There, Freddie produced two local fruit juices – a strangely pink apple, and ginger. Both were exquisite – and just what we needed. First he played us some of his songs: 'Reggae's a music, a feel,' he told us, 'and it's been created right here on this island of Jamaica over the last fifty years or so by people like Toots and the Maytals and Bob Marley. Like Bob Marley said, you feel reggae in the one drop – it's a beat that people respond to in a way that sometimes surprises me. It arrived just after ska, which is real fast, and rock steady, which is slower, and we've been rocking the world with reggae ever since.'

All of the Caribbean islands have developed different musical styles and Freddie believes that reggae has its roots in African music. 'When I travel to the different islands and hear different accents, different rhythmic beats, I'm like, wow, how did this happen? We're all the same people, and that leads me to think that different people on different islands were probably from different parts of Africa. I think Jamaican people are from West Africa, and when we started working on the plantations we had to find a way to release our stress so we sang.'

In the 1960s, reggae was the voice of a new generation, forming its own identity in Jamaica. The lyrics express social discontent: they protest against poverty and government oppression, to awaken class-consciousness. Music is the heartbeat of Jamaica – you hear it wherever you go – and during the 1970s and 1980s, reggae provided the ideal means for Rastafarianism to send its message of resistance around the world. Jamaica might once have been famous for slavery but it is now known to the world for its music.

When we left Freddie, we followed a modern metalled road out of the city, into a lush green landscape of palms, bananas and sugarcane. We were keen to visit one of the old plantations to get a sense of how they were once run. The long drive up through Barnett Estates leading to Bellefield Great House gave us an idea of the scale of the operation. At one time the estate included fifty thousand acres of sugar plantation, but the landholding is now reduced to around three thousand, growing sugarcane, mangoes, coconuts, bananas, other tropical fruits and flowers. The house is a magnificent example of eighteenth-century colonial architecture and has been carefully restored as a museum. The old sugar mill is now a restaurant. Built in white stone with a slate roof over-hanging the first-floor balcony, it has a small formal garden, complete with a fountain that seems very English.

We stood on the dark wood balcony with Aleric Josephs, a lecturer from the University of the West Indies, who was our guide to the plantation. She took care to be precise in what she told us, but every now and then we'd catch a flash of her smile. 'When the British arrived,' she said, 'there were already slaves here under Spanish rule. There weren't enough white indentured servants to work the plantations so the British decided to use blacks.' The slaves were bought at auction or from a 'scramble': they would stand in a group and the planters would rush in to grab the ones they wanted. 'That was probably the most frightening experience in terms of sale.' Then they were taken to the plantation where they would be 'seasoned', or put to work with trained slaves to learn about planta-tion life from them.

'If the owner was resident, he would live in the great house,' Aleric explained. 'If he lived overseas, he would have a manager or "attorney" who acted in his absence. The attorney oversaw the whole thing and might even be in charge of more than one estate. In addition, he'd have an overseer who lived in a separate house and looked after the day-to-day running of the plantation. The workers lived in small huts near the fields. There was usually a slave village on each plantation where all the field workers congregated while the domestic slaves lived in the great house.

'The days were very long, especially in crop time,' Aleric continued. 'The mills were running all night so slaves might work up to sixteen hours a day because they would have to harvest a lot of cane. During crop time, from December to May, they would be mainly cutting it with machetes and carting it to the mill. During the off season, they would be replanting, weeding, manuring, fixing the fences and so on, as well as repairing any damage to the mill and the factory buildings.'

We wondered if the slaves were ever allowed any time off. 'On Sundays they used to go to the markets near the plantations,' Aleric explained. 'They would do a lot of socialising there and sell their own produce from the "provision grounds". They'd also get special holidays, like Christmas, and at the end of crop time they got a few days for celebration.' As the slave owners tried to erase the cultural identity of their slaves, the markets, newly arrived slaves, and the practice in secret of traditional rituals and healing, kept it alive.

The slave population was supposed to reproduce constantly, thus replenishing the labour force, but apparently, whenever they could, women would abort their babies or persuade the midwife to kill a newborn rather than allow it to live as a slave. 'That's why slavery became so expensive: the owners had to keep on buying more and as demand increased, the price went up.'

Living conditions varied, depending on who was in charge of the estate. 'There are stories of slaves rebelling because the conditions weren't good or they weren't getting adequate food, but the punishments were very harsh.' The only successful rebellion that Aleric could recall took place in Haiti where the government was overthrown and a black republic set up. Otherwise rebellious slaves might set fire to a plantation or conduct a campaign of constant sabotage, either by working slowly, by poisoning animals, or damaging equipment.

But life for the planters and their families, some of whom were a long way from home, was also far from easy, and by the second half of the eighteenth century many plantations had been abandoned. 'It would take another twelve to fifteen months to get the fields in operation again,' said Aleric, 'and often that meant borrowing money. Historians believe that this led to the ultimate demise of slavery, because by the second half of the eighteenth century many plantations were in serious financial trouble.' In Aleric's opinion, industrialisation and the evangelical revival in Britain combined to bring about the end of slavery. 'Some owners returned to England. Some plantations were sold cheaply, and others remained in operation into the twentieth century, sold to companies like Tate and Lyle or the United Food Company.'

~ Rough Justice ~

Jamaica was no place to enjoy your wealth. There was the ever-present threat of disease, such as yellow fever, but also the white population was outnumbered twenty to one by the slaves. They lived in constant terror of revolt and massacre. Fear drove the 'plantocracy' to violence: punishments included flogging, amputation and castration; a common method of execution was burning to death over a slow fire, which began at the feet and moved up the body.

One owner, the famous diarist William Hickey, was so enraged when an overseer flogged a girl that he had the man arrested. The next day the culprit was shot while attempting to escape. It was a form of rough justice.

The 1760 rising: rich planters lived in constant
fear of slave rebellion

Brutality did not prevent the slaves becoming 'saucy'. In 1760 hundreds rebelled, causing the deaths of sixty whites and more than a thousand slaves.

∾ Black-Coated Revolutionaries ∾

When the evangelists arrived on the island in the nineteenth century, their work was far from straightforward. 'No Englishman, except a missionary, would be treated with such contempt' was Thomas Burchell's description of his treatment by Jamaican society. Burchell, James Phillippo and William Knibb, were ministers from the Baptist Foreign Missionary Society posted to the island in the 1820s. Their message was that the slaves 'were destined to occupy the same rank with ourselves in the great family of man'. This was calculated to horrify the planters, who were already worried by the existence of a Native Baptist Church, founded by American slaves freed by the British during the revolutionary wars. Not only were Baptists working-class and dangerously democratic, their religious practices were sympathetic to African traditions. There were wonderful hymns, and the central Baptist rite was incomparably dramatic: the entire congregation, singing and shouting, accompanied the pastor and the new member, clad in white, to the sea, in which their sins were washed away and they were welcomed into the warmth of a new fellowship. Baptist missionaries taught both Christianity and democratic debate to small classes under the direction of pastors and elders, in the Methodist tradition.

In May 1831 rumours reached the island that a new Whig government in Britain had abolished slavery. When the governor issued an official denial, the disappointment was too much for the slaves of Montego Bay, where the senior Baptist deacon and slave, 'Daddy' Samuel Sharpe, was in charge during Pastor Burchell's absence in Britain. Sharpe seems to have planned for some form of general strike but that was not enough to satisfy the slaves, who burst into rebellion, shouting, 'Nigger man, nigger man, burn the house – burn buckra house! Brimstone come! Bring fire and burn Massa house!'

Twenty thousand slaves had attacked more than two hundred plantations before the revolt was crushed. Some fourteen whites and two hundred slaves and 'free blacks' (emancipated slaves and immigrants) were killed. Immediately the planters' supporters turned on the missionaries, burning down their chapels and threatening to lynch them; the Reverend Henry Bleby was tarred and about to be set ablaze when he was rescued. The Governor did nothing to prevent the violence, but official revenge was summary: six hundred and twenty-six rebels were tried and three hundred and twelve hanged, including some free blacks and two whites.

Sharpe was one of those condemned. Accompanied by Bleby, he went to the scaffold 'with a firm and even dignified step, clothed in a suit of new white clothes'. He became a national hero; his owner was paid £16.10s. as compensation for the loss of his property.

The 'Baptist War' was a precipitating factor in the abolition of slavery. It had not been too difficult to put an end to the trade but the institution was more resilient. British governments questioned their constitutional authority to override the colonists' wishes. Jamaica's legislature had managed the island's affairs for more than a hundred-and-seventy years, and some planters considered declaring independence rather than accept abolition. The economic consequences of changing the labour system were grave, and the cost of compensating the owners was enormous – it amounted to £20 million. William Knibb returned to Britain to stimulate action; in Liverpool, when he heard that the Reform Bill had become law, he exclaimed, 'Thank God! Now I'll have slavery down.'

It was another year before the Abolition Bill was pushed through Parliament, but from 1 August 1834 slavery became illegal throughout the British Empire. In Jamaica, as midnight on 31 July drew near, Knibb's congregation sang:

'The death blow is struck – see the monster is dying,
He cannot survive till the dawn streaks the sky;
In one single hour, he will prostrate be lying,
Come, shout o'er the grave where so soon he will lie.'

∾ England's Worst Crime ∾

John Wesley's anti-slavery pamphlet, 'Thoughts upon Slavery', published in 1774, drew attention to Britain's 'worst crime'. Not only the Methodists but many Anglicans now formed a wide 'evangelical' and humanitarian alliance.

The unlikely trigger for anti-slavery agitation was a Latin prize essay, submitted in 1784 by Thomas Clarkson, a Cambridge undergraduate, whose research had convinced him of the wickedness of slavery. His essay attracted the notice of his contemporary William Wilberforce, Tory MP for Hull, and his friend, the young Tory prime minister, William Pitt.

By 1787 Clarkson had established the 'Committee for Effecting the Abolition of the Slave Trade'. Frustrated by the slave owners' parliamentary supporters and still more by the general horror of change inspired by the French Revolution, implementation was delayed. Finally, in January 1807, the Abolition of Slavery Act was passed by an impressive Commons majority of two hundred and eighty-three to sixteen. Britain could claim to have been last into the slave trade and first out – but during the century and a half that she had engaged in it, she had been responsible for enslaving more than three million Africans.

In Jamaica, the slave owners were horrified. With no prospect of renewing their stock, commercial survival depended on their existing slaves. British governments attempted to persuade them to improve conditions and gradually develop a paid workforce, but the Jamaican Assembly chose to impose even harsher disciplines. Debating whether women should be flogged 'decently' (clothed) or 'indecently' (naked), they opted for the latter: it was more exciting for the spectators.

By this time the Assembly, elected by around eight hundred voters, far from represented the population – then some 370,000, of whom only 16,000 were white and 65,000 Coloured. Many of the Coloureds were already reasonably prosperous and were becoming influential. Edward Jordan, who later became the first premier of Jamaica, founded the influential *Watchman* newspaper in 1829. The slaves would have to wait another generation before they were officially acknowledged as humans, but the Coloureds were certain to dominate any properly representative government – and, when eventually a reforming Whig government was elected, that was only a matter of time.

GHANA

The main road from Accra to Assin Manso, on the first stage of our trip to Assin Manso. Shopping as far as you can see.

Local children play in the harbour as the fishing boats return to Elmina, Ghana.

Assin Manso – hard to enjoy the beauty once you are told this was where slaves were washed to make them more appealing to traders.

The slaves would have walked this path leading to the river at Assin Manso to have their last bath before being marched on to Cape Coast.

A mural at Slave River depicts slaves being washed before being sold.

Adjekulai tells me the story of the slaves' terrible journey.

It was between these trees that slaves were tied prior to the long walk to Cape Coast.

Ghanaian children play on the beach in front of Cape Coast Castle.

All this fire power to protect the British community from innocent stolen Africans.

The Door of No Return. Slaves were led through the door and onto the boats, never to see Africa again.

Looking out of the Door of No Return. Slave traders and their ships would have waited here for their human cargo. Now it is a peaceful harbour for fishermen.

Queen Victoria overlooking the park named after her, which, like any park in Britain, is full of rubbish and old carrier bags.

Can you find me in this picture?

Nana and Imahkus Ofoku – the former fireman and travel agent who feel Ghana is their spiritual home.

The rugged and magnificent Ghana coast. Even here the temperature never dropped below the mid-thirties.

However, life immediately after emancipation was still hard. Field workers had another six years' apprenticeship to work and artisans another four. Working hours were reduced to forty a week but the planters were anxious to see the same amount of work done. 'In one sense, apprenticeship was as hard as slavery,' Aleric told us. 'But the missionaries campaigned for it to end early. When it came there was grand celebration.'

The social structure didn't change immediately. 'Blacks were free on paper but they were at the bottom of the social ladder, and the majority were still plantation workers. The missionaries helped to ease the pressure through church activities and providing education of a sort. But the social structure remained the same: if you are white, you are at the top; if you are black you are the bottom; the middle would be the mixed group of coloureds.'

Emancipation marked a change in the crops that were grown. 'This was often initiated by the former slaves who, helped by the missionaries, bought land and became peasant farmers who diversified the economy by planting different things. The labour force continued to be largely black but other people were brought in as contract labour from Asia, China and India.' Aleric also spoke of a resurgence in African Caribbean practices that had been restricted during slavery: 'In fact one historian said that we actually saw two Jamaicas emerging by the 1850s: the Euro-Jamaican and the Afro-Jamaican. The divide was noticeable for a very long time.'

∼ Free Villages ∼

Samuel and Edward Barrett were leading figures in early-nineteenth-century Jamaica. Samuel was master of the extensive family estates and attempted to squeeze rents out of every man, woman and even child living on his land; Edward was a freed slave who had been named after his owner. Edward, an accountant and Baptist deacon, was presented to the British public as 'the archetypical new black subject: the responsible, industrious, Christian man'. But most freemen were not like Edward Barrett.

As many had predicted, serious problems followed emancipation. Lord Harris, Governor of Trinidad in 1846, lamented that 'A race has been freed, but a society has not been formed.' Adult agricultural slaves were not to become independent immediately, but had to continue to work for their former masters as paid 'apprentices' for up to six years – this condition was dropped in 1838. But the last thing many freed slaves wanted was to return to the hardship of the plantations. Deprived of cheap labour the planters were desperate: one Jamaican estate valued at £80,000 before abolition sold for only £500 fifteen years later.

Black progress was unsteady too. British abolitionists and Jamaican missionaries assumed that slaves would develop naturally into sober, diligent and responsible wage-earners, but many rejected this ideal, insisting instead on their African heritage. The Baptists preached equality, but the white pastors lived in substantial manses well away from the slave huts. Christianity taught patient suffering until the final triumph of good; the slaves knew all too well the reality of human evil.

After 1834, Blacks and Coloureds were enfranchised on the same basis as whites. They could elect members to the legislature and participate in the island's government, the executive committee. In British colonies the right to vote was not primarily a matter of race but of class, which often came to the same thing, with the franchise given only to property owners. The missionaries therefore began an imaginative programme to purchase estates for division among their congregations, who would then have an economic stake in the country, and political rights.

James Phillippo introduced the 'free village' programme in October 1835 with Sligo, named after a sympathetic former governor. William Knibb followed, borrowing money in England to buy five hundred acres of good land. Again, his villages bore the names of allies: Clarkson, Wilberforce and Victoria, for the Queen was seen as the ultimate source of justice. By 1840 eight thousand families were living in the free villages, developing the Baptist model of citizenship, assisted by schools, a training college named Calabar, friendly societies and savings banks. Not all succeeded. The right to vote depended on the continued payment of land taxes, with which many new freeholders fell behind, and the registration formalities were complex, which discouraged the illiterate. Of the eight thousand who should have been entitled to vote by mid-century, fewer than two thousand registered.

Even after the final abolition of any form of servitude in 1838 the plantocracy fought back, and brought down Lord Melbourne's government. But neither Whigs nor Tories could solve Jamaica's problems without the assembly's co-operation in amending what Gladstone called its 'vicious constitution'.

The jubilation slowly dissipated in a cloud of disillusion. Representative government meant little to the majority of Blacks, who saw whites and Coloureds, the plantocracy and the urban middle class, running the country as it suited them. The charismatic old leaders left the scene. By 1845 Knibb had succumbed to yellow fever, and Thomas Burchell died the following year. Only Phillippo remained, a venerated figure, who acknowledged that there remained much work to do before his ideals could be realised. In 1859 Anthony Trollope, visiting the island, wrote that 'It is one of the few sores on our huge and healthy carcase' and described Kingston 'like the city of the dead'.

The sun was going down as we headed towards the hills in the centre of the island. Soon we turned off the main road on to a dirt track. The only direction we had to Victoria Town was to turn left at a pile of tyres. We followed the dusty red track for some distance, past occasional farms, and at the tyres turned up into Victoria, a linear town that runs through the hills, consisting of pleasant modern houses of varying sizes, painted in pastel colours, each with a little veranda and a tin roof; everywhere was lightly overgrown with lush, large-leafed vegetation. A misty hush had descended on the town – it had been raining earlier – and the hills created a strange acoustic distortion: we could hear the radios of cars far in the distance. It was like a ghost town, empty except for one or two elderly men sitting contemplatively on their porches.

We soon discovered why. When the pastor took us into his small, aquamarine-decorated church, many of the

townsfolk were waiting there. They had arranged to per-
form the Bruckins Dance for us. The dance celebrates the
end of the slave trade and is now reserved for festivals or
competitions. Several children, aged between five and fifteen, were sitting in a corner, half of them in brilliant blue
and the rest in red. Their elaborate costumes represent
British characters – kings, queens, courtiers, sergeant-
majors and captains. Each side tries to out-dance the
other; the songs offer thanks to Queen Victoria for freeing
the slaves. Suddenly another group of children struck up
a drum beat and those in costume began to sing at the
tops of their voices. The simple melody and repetitive
beat sounded to us more like African music than the
reggae, or dub, we had heard earlier that day. Watching
the performers in the middle of the floor, with their
unfamiliar short sharp movements, was electrifying. They
danced for five minutes, shoulders and hips popping.

Jubilee, jubilee, this is the year of the jubilee,
August mawnin' cum again,
August mawnin' cum again.

The children put their hearts and souls into their dance
while the audience of proud mums and dads, and us,
clapped to the rhythm. It was one of the most memorable
and moving nights of our trip.

Outside the church, night had fallen and the forest was
coming to life with the chirping of crickets, cicadas and
other unseen creatures. We were sorry to leave, suspecting
that the children would go on dancing into the night.

∼ Ominous Hats ∼

The free villages survived, but a prosperous peasantry failed to materialise. Land remained unused, but capital to buy it was scarce and many people did not even know it was for sale. A petition in April 1865 asked, 'Our Gracious Lady Queen Victoria' to appoint an agent to receive local farmers' produce: 'We will put our hands and hearts to work and cultivate coffee, corn, cocoa, cotton and tobacco', if someone would help them sell it. The Queen never saw the petition, which remained in the Colonial Office, and those who had signed it were told that, like British workers, they should take whatever jobs they could get.

Blacks had been let down by political institutions, so less formal groupings began to exercise power. Organised strikes or 'riotous bargaining', such as Sam Sharpe had planned, led to concessions being granted. The Native Baptist Church grew, its congregations electing their own pastors and deacons. For some years a sensible executive committee, which included two planters and a Coloured merchant, worked with an experienced governor (Sir Henry Barkly) to achieve stability, but this stability did not survive the Governor's departure in 1856.

One magistrate saw trouble coming: the Blacks had taken to wearing hats 'at least two feet and six inches in diameter, in which no man could work' – but when discontent erupted into another violent protest in Morant Bay it came as a shock.

In the Native Baptist chapel of Paul Bogle, a deacon and prosperous farmer, the protest was brief but fierce. Two planters and eighteen other whites were beaten to death

The Morant Bay Revolt

before it was suppressed by troops and the ever-willing Maroons, the community of former slaves who had allied themselves with the government. The brutal suppression of the revolt, ordered by Governor Edward Eyre, sparked widespread indignation in Britain – Eyre's illegal order for the arrest and trial of George Gordon, a coloured assembly member, by a hastily convened court headed by a junior naval officer of clearly sadistic tendencies, was especially scandalous. Lieutenant Herbert Brand of HMS *Onyx* ordered that a hundred and twenty-two men and four women should be publicly hanged; the women were 'of the worst class only, such as Judy Edwards or Letitia Geoghegan, who, with her four sons, was executed'. Only seven of those tried were acquitted.

Britain was divided on the question of the governor's responsibility: some who defended Edward Eyre, who had been a distinguished Australian explorer, and others who were horrified by his conduct. J. S. Mill and Thomas Huxley led the attack, while Charles Dickens, Lord Tennyson and John Ruskin founded the Eyre Defence Committee. Eventually Eyre was pensioned off and the naval officers involved were allowed to slink into obscurity, but Jamaica's independent legislature was persuaded to abolish itself in favour of direct rule from London as a Crown Colony.

That night we stayed at Treasure Beach, where six miles of white-sand beaches and rocky coves are strung between a series of quiet fishing villages. It is on the coast of the parish of St Elizabeth, known as the 'breadbasket of Jamaica' because it provides more fruit and vegetables to the island than any other parish even though it has the lowest rainfall.

The following morning we went to a nearby beauty spot known as Lovers' Leap, where it is said an enslaved couple leapt to their death rather than face separation, or that a girl leapt into the sea in a vain attempt to join her true love, who was sailing away from the island. We found a café there, with a balcony that overlooks a breathtaking drop thousands of feet to the sea below where the deep blue water turned to jade green then aquamarine.

∿ A Proud People ∿

The 'Maroons', escaped slaves who had formed their own communities in the mountains, were a potential ally for the planters. Doggedly independent, they defied authority until a formal treaty with the Jamaican Government was made in 1739. Maroon headmen were awarded military titles and silver badges of office, and invited to Government House. A proud race, they were deeply offended when, in 1795, two of them were flogged for stealing pigs; a full-scale war against British forces was only ended when the British commander, Colonel George Walpole, guaranteed that the Maroons would not be punished and would be allowed to remain on the island. When the governor, Lord Balcarres, reneged on the terms of the treaty, Walpole objected furiously but hundreds of Maroons were exiled, first to Nova Scotia and thence to the new African colony of Sierra Leone.

The next day, which was damp and overcast, found us heading into the mountains. The road wound round steep-sided valleys often overlooking a terrifyingly sheer drop. Then, all of a sudden, the view would disappear into the thick cloud that clung to rich green forests. The landscape stretched away below and the higher we climbed, the lower the temperature fell until we were reaching for jumpers and jackets. The town of Accompong seemed to come from nowhere: one or two houses built on the slopes gradually swelled into a rural high street.

Most of the inhabitants had gathered to meet us in the central hall, then led us through the back of the village and down a couple of hundred metres of muddy path to the kindah tree – kindah meaning 'one family' – an ancient mango tree whose vast branches shaded the rocky ground. The view stretched for miles across the lush green of Cock Pit country, but that day low cloud obscured much of it.

A respectful silence fell over the townspeople as we were welcomed by a man covered with leaves, a demonstration of the camouflage used against the British almost three hundred years ago. As he spoke, mist swirled around the tree, throwing the green leaves into sharp relief, intensifying the ethereal atmosphere: 'We have Ashanti, Cromanti and Conga tribes living in this community. When the British and Spanish freed the slaves or they escaped, they came to the hills for refuge and returned to their tribes, which fought each other. In the early seventeenth century, the tribal leaders met under this tree and concluded that they were one people fighting for the same cause so they must unite. They pricked the arteries of their hands, let the blood flow into a bowl, mixed it with some rum and drank it in the name of peace and brotherhood.' Then in a gesture of welcome, another man poured rum into our hands, which we rubbed over our faces.

Every year, on 6 January, Accompong marks the birthday of Cudjoe, the great Maroon leader who brokered the 1739 peace treaty between his people and the British. Thousands of people descend on the village which rocks all day to the sound of drumming and the abeng, a cow's horn, which was once blown to warn neighbouring tribes that enemies were approaching. The Maroons have kept themselves and their culture distinct from that of the rest of the island; their distinctive dancing and singing culminate in a grand procession to the kindah tree. A small group of women in white bandannas and shirts with red-and-white checked skirts performed a dance for us, singing to the beat of drums and the sound of the horn.

The Maroons have maintained their independence into the twenty-first century, and do not even pay Jamaican taxes. As we sat under the kindah, we met their colonel, elected into his second five-year term of office as leader of their government. 'We are proud of what our ancestors did,' he told us. 'Imagine a bunch of blacks in the bush waging a successful war against Britain, the most power-ful nation in the world at that time, and forcing a treaty. It's something to be proud of.'

He went on to talk about a colourful character in his people's history: Nanny of the Maroons, the only female among Jamaica's national heroes and sister (or possibly mother) of Cudjoe. She led them between 1725 and 1740, some of the most turbulent years in their history, and was a skilled guerrilla fighter. It was said she could catch bullets in her hands, but some believe she caught them between her buttocks and blew them out again.

According to the Colonel, the Maroons are still aware of the difference between themselves and other Jamaicans: 'We feel it in spirit, in everything. We remem-ber where we came from and keep alive certain traditions that the rest of Jamaica comes to see, like our dancing, our food and some of our customs.' The Colonel had lived in Britain during the 1960s and 1970s, working on buses and trains: 'In the beginning we had problems getting a place to live. But there was lots of work so we didn't meet any dreadful discrimination. Possibly I was lucky. I worked hard so they got to like me, and then I didn't have much problem with the British.'

Jamaica is a beautiful island – as the tour brochures show – and its people are committed to building a future and a strong new identity for their country. It has problems, but is searching for ways to solve them. Where Ghana felt as though it carried a heavy yoke on its back, because its people have not yet been able to escape the injustices of their past, in Jamaica, the mood was different – people were shouting, 'Yes! We did it. You didn't destroy us. Now we're going to live.'

3

Newfoundland

It was a real relief to get to St Johns after Ghana and Jamaica – just to be somewhere cold. It was chilly, rainy and foggy, but I'm from Lancashire, you can't scare me. We'd come to look at the story of the transatlantic cable – the wire that changed the world: the first successful underwater cable was laid in the sea bed between Ireland and Newfoundland. They said it was so flat and with so few underwater currents it could have been designed with the cable in mind. Without the telegraph the Empire could never have grown so quickly, and the British government would never have been able to control so many far-flung places.

I was really excited about going to the museum in the morning and seeing a bit of the actual cable. To make it waterproof the core was protected with gutta-percha, a rubbery substance from the gum of the Malaysian gutta tree. The gum is a sort of natural plastic that can be moulded at high temperatures, and is still flexible when it cools. Gutta-percha arrived in Britain in 1843, and the Gutta Percha Company was founded two years later, but as the transatlantic cable wouldn't be needed for some years, they filled in the time making tea trays, golf balls and ear trumpets.

I had hopes of filming something about gutta percha when we went to Borneo, but nothing doing – I got stuck with sago. Defend sago as you will, you must admit no one has ever made a tea tray out of it.

As I've said, we were always on a very tight schedule, and we needed our interviewees to be on the ball. We didn't have time for them to hesitate or deviate from the subject – it was like doing *Just A Minute* without the laughs. As someone who can't bear to be late, I found it really painful to be doing an interview in one location, knowing that somewhere else another interviewee was waiting for us to arrive, but short of shouting 'For god's sake will you talk quicker?' there wasn't much to be done.

We had arranged to film at a bonfire party some miles out of St Johns, once we had finished our interview with Carla, the monarchist, and her friend who made figurines of members of the Royal Family. We thought the party would look great on film, and there was going to be lots of traditional music.

The whole monarchy interview took a time to get going, and I never did really pin down why someone would want to cram their house to the gunwales with Lady Di plates and mugs covered with grumpy old royal faces. By the time we got to the bonfire, the fire was out, the rain was beating down, nearly everyone had left, and the ones who had stayed were cross, wet, and half of them were English anyway. Bah.

We all felt much better in the cool of Newfoundland, but I was the only one who had to eat the sixteenth-century food prepared by two ladies in costume who re-created the diet of the very first English settlers. I already felt a bit sick, and the sight of two ladies in mob-caps bending over a small smoky fire and stirring something sludgy in a black iron cauldron didn't make me feel any friskier. We shot a whole sequence, with me eating as little as possible and trying to ask intelligent questions. Though all I really wanted to do was run in, shout, 'Angel Delight!' and run out again. Then I was asked to repeat the sequence so it could be shot from a different angle. And if you want to know what's less appetising to a person with a stomach bug than barley cooked in white wine and butter, it's cold barley cooked in white wine and butter.

~ *Introduction* ~

Since the fifteenth century the British had been attracted to Newfoundland by the teeming cod fisheries of the Grand Banks but put off by the harsh winters. Formal government was only established there in the early nineteenth century, two hundred years after the first settlers arrived. The defence of their fishing rights against French and American encroachment, together with an independent spirit, stopped Newfoundland joining Canada in the 1860s; she finally bowed to economic pressure in 1949. Today Canada, with Australia, is one of the world's most advanced large countries.

We arrived in Newfoundland very early in the morning, to be slapped in the face by the freezing air. As the sun rose, the unforgiving landscape presented a sharp contrast to the sunshine, balmy beaches, and tropical forests of Jamaica. The scenery was dramatic and the seascapes spectacular. While we were on the island, though, the weather never let up. Leaden cloud covered the sky. Rain and wind lashed the coast, bringing with them a heavy sea mist. According to Canada's Atlantic weather centre, Newfoundland's capital city, St John's, is the foggiest, wettest, snowiest, windiest and cloudiest of all Canada's major cities. They also report that native Newfoundlanders regard their climate as 'character-building' and 'invigorating'.

Outside St John's, small fishing communities of painted weatherboard houses huddle together, facing out towards the grey ocean from which generations of Newfoundlanders have clawed a precarious living.

～ *The First Nation* ～

The first serious attempt to colonise Newfoundland was made, probably in 1002, by an Icelander, Thorfinn Karlsevni. His crew found grapes and wild wheat, and passed a mild winter on the island – the northern climate was less challenging a thousand years ago, – before they were attacked by the locals, or skraelings, as the Norse called them. They were saved only by Freydis, Erik the Red's daughter, 'who bared her breasts, slapped them with a sword and screamed like a hellcat', which frightened the locals off.

The skraelings were probably the ancestors of the Beotuk, who inhabited the island five hundred years later. In mainland Canada the 'Indians', now known as the First Nations, were generally strong and united enough to survive persecution, but the Beotuk of Newfoundland have disappeared. They numbered around five hundred at most, too few to absorb the stresses of imported disease and interference with their way of life.

In 1501 the Portuguese captured fifty-seven 'Red Indians' – so-called for the ochre with which they decorated their bodies and described them as 'living altogether by fishing and hunting animals in which the land abounds . . . Their manners and gestures are most gentle; they laugh considerably and manifest the greatest pleasure . . . The women have small breasts and most beautiful bodies, and rather pleasant faces.' They would, the Portuguese decided, make useful slaves. French writers were less complimentary: 'a cruel and rude people with whom we can neither deal or converse'.

After that, the Beotuk kept away from the coasts and were safe until British settlers moved inland and hunted them down. The last Beotuk, a girl named Shanadithit, died in 1829, leaving some remarkable drawings, which give a hint of her people's culture.

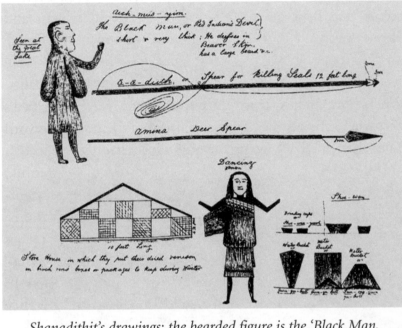

Shanadithit's drawings: the bearded figure is the 'Black Man, or the Indian's Devil'

We had heard about the harsh life the first settlers endured, so the island's geography was no surprise. We anticipated taking a step back in time to the sort of fishing communities that once peppered the coasts of Cornwall or Western Ireland. We assumed this would be the most British of the places we would visit on our journey round the empire – a cold rock stuck in the Atlantic and close to a major continent sounded just like home! As the first British overseas colony, we expected to find a population whose links to Britain and Ireland through family ties, commerce, political life or trade, would be strong.

Actually, the first link between Britain and its new colony was fish.

❧ *A Fishy Business* ❧

When despatches from Newfoundland reached Queen Victoria's officials they were usually about fish. The recorded history of what may be Britain's oldest colony began with

Cod fishing on the Grand Banks

quarrels over fish. These took place between Britain, France and the USA throughout the nineteenth century. The Queen's reign ended amid a storm of controversy as to whether or not lobsters were fish.

Fishing began on the Grand Banks, the shallow waters that stretch two hundred miles or so to the south and east of Newfoundland. Since the early fifteenth century Basques,

Salting freshly-killed cod

Bretons and Normans had exploited them. The navigator John Cabot, of Bristol, reported the results of his North American voyage to King Henry VII in 1497, describing shoals of cod so thick that sometimes they 'stayed his ship'. The cod were caught on long lines, then salted and dried for storage, to provide essential winter protein for the home ports. Fishing was limited to the summer because the

Newfoundland winter was dangerously cold and inhospitable. The fishermen landed to repair their tackle and dry the fish, but they never built a permanent settlement.

Cabot's reports were not followed up – London merchants were suspicious of those based in Bristol – and neither the Dutch nor the British, both of whom had an extensive fishing fleet, showed much interest in Grand Banks cod. After all, they had an abundant supply of herring in the North Sea. But cod was cheap and easy to store – it can be thrown about like firewood without coming to harm – which meant that it eventually found a place in British markets.

The first item on our itinerary was a visit to Victoria Park in St John's, which is considered the oldest settlement in North America and was named by John Cabot. It is a small city that hugs a stunning natural harbour, flanked by vast cliffs. Traditional pastel-painted weatherboard houses line streets that rise up the surrounding craggy hills, interspersed with a few high-rises. The Basilica of St John's, the imposing Roman Catholic cathedral built between 1841 and 1850, stands high on Military Road overlooking the harbour.

∼ Britain's Oldest Colony ∼

Newfoundland's claim to be Britain's oldest colony originates in a charter given in 1578 by Queen Elizabeth I to Sir Humphrey Gilbert, which entitled him to occupy any lands between Labrador and Florida 'not actually possessed of any

Christian prince or people'. Settlers were to enjoy all the rights and privileges of Englishmen 'as if they were born and personally resident in the said realm'.

Sir Humphrey's 1583 expedition to Newfoundland was a failure. He had a well-equipped fleet, which included trumpeters, drummers, morris dancers and hobbyhorses to entertain the colonists, and Parmenius, a learned Hungarian, to record the voyage, but he spent less than a month on the coast of Newfoundland before he

An elegant Sir Humphrey Gilbert at St. John's

returned to England. Parmenius gloomily noted, '*Praeter solitudinem nihil video. Piscium inexausta copia.*' 'Nothing to be seen but solitude and a great deal of fish.' But the British flag had been planted at St John's on 5 August 1583, and might be said to have marked the foundation of what became the British Empire.

In 1610 the Bristol brothers John and Philip Guy proposed to 'animate the English to plant in Newfoundland' and succeeded in establishing a colony of forty hardy settlers, which struggled on for some years. In 1621 Sir George Calvert began a more ambitious project to establish a village in the southern part of Newfoundland, an area he called Avalon.

Nowhere on the island is further than a hundred kilometres from the sea, and life has always been dominated by the fishery. Today merchant ships, tankers, cruise-ships and fishing vessels fill the harbour. At night two sets of red lights shine out over the city to guide ships between the cliffs that protect it from the elements. We watched some leave the port, amazed by the battering they took as they headed into the open sea. What could it have been like for the first fishermen in their little boats?

∽ Worth More Than the Whole of Canada ∽

Come, cheer up, my lads! 'tis to glory we steer,
To add something more to this wonderful year.

1759 was the 'wonderful year' to which David Garrick referred: Britain had driven the French out of Canada, fought a triumphant battle against the French at Minden, prevented an invasion of England by annihilating the French fleet at Quiberon Bay, and captured the wealthy sugar island of Guadeloupe.

Peace negotiations began two years later and dragged on for another two, as debate raged over which conquests the British should retain. The French were stubbornly reluctant to surrender the fisheries, which one French minister insisted were 'worth more than the whole of Canada'.

The final treaty transferred all of Canada to Britain, with the exception of two tiny islands off the coast of Newfoundland: St Pierre and Miquelon, which are still French today, with a population of six-and-a-half thousand. However, French fishing rights were extended to cover

---

nearly half of the Newfoundland coast, with the opposite section of the Labrador mainland.

There was little the British government could do to enforce this unpopular agreement, and there were frequent disputes. During the summer season the naval commander also acted as governor, appointing magistrates to keep order among the settlers as the fishing admiral did among the sailors. Since Newfoundland was not much smaller than Britain, with a population in 1800 of some twenty thousand, the only justice available was rough and ready.

The slow movement towards adoption of a formal colonial constitution began in 1792, with the foundation of a Supreme Court. Civilian governors were appointed from 1825, and in 1832 an assembly was elected to govern the island. It was to run on British lines, with the governor representing the monarch, the executive council (or governing body) commanding a majority in the Legislative Assembly, and the Legislative Council having powers similar to those of the House of Lords. This model was the template for self-government in all 'settlement' colonies. Since by that time some forty per cent of the population were Irish Catholics, who were frequently at odds with the Protestants, Newfoundland's early governments were chaotic. Religious divisions led to electoral violence, and endless disputes between the Assembly, which was often Catholic, and the Council which was almost exclusively Protestant. While in Ireland Catholics formed a substantial majority, in Newfoundland the churches were more evenly balanced, making compromise inevitable. In 1854 Newfoundland became, like the other Canadian provinces, independent in all matters apart from foreign policy.

Looking inland, our initial plan had been to visit Victoria Park, but the rain was lashing down so hard that we could barely walk in a straight line. Instead we went straight to Signal Hill, a look-out point east of St John's with a commanding view of the town and the ocean – when the mist clears. Cabot Tower, a distinctive stone building with a fifty-foot octagonal tower at its south-east corner, was constructed there in 1897 to commemorate the four hundredth anniversary of Cabot's arrival, and Queen Victoria's diamond jubilee. It was used for flag signalling until 1957 when the hill became a National Historic Site of Canada. Flags told townspeople and the militia that a ship was approaching and also of a wreck, when men would take their boats out to help. Just below Cabot Tower, Ladies' Look-out is the spot where anxious wives gathered to wait for their men to come home from fishing. We couldn't help thinking of those who had crossed the wild sea below us to reach the island and had endured the conditions, and worse, that we were experiencing. They must have been desperate to leave.

At Cabot Tower, we met Alistair Black, an enthusiastic amateur radio operator who works at the local communications museum. As we looked out at the drenching rain and mist, he told us of the significant role Newfoundland had played in the history of communications. The view over the Atlantic makes you feel as though you are on the edge of nowhere, but this area of North America is nearer to Dublin than it is to Toronto, and the natural destination for a communications cable from Britain.

'Newfoundland was half-way between the old world and the new,' Alistair said. 'Communications were changing everything. There were cables across Europe and the Americas. The link across the Atlantic was the last piece. Before the telegraph, the quickest way of getting a message from Great Britain to here was by ship. That took about two weeks, or nine days if they had favourable winds.' He showed us a piece of the first thin cable that was laid under water in 1858 between Valentia Island in western Ireland and Trinity Bay, Newfoundland. 'It's a type of galvanised steel with a core for passing the message. Later cables were more sophisticated but in the early days it was difficult to send a message all the way down. They would overload the electrical power as they tried to force the message down the wire and the cable would break.'

There had been several failed attempts to establish this link in international communications, and hundreds of miles of expensive cable were lost at the bottom of the Atlantic. Undeterred, on 29 July 1858 two converted naval steamships, Niagara and Agamemnon, rendezvoused in mid-ocean, each loaded with more than a thousand miles of telegraphic cable. The cable was spliced together, then lowered with special equipment to the sea-bed, two thousand fathoms below. That done, the ships moved away from each other, paying out the cable. Eight days later Agamemnon reached Valentia and Niagara berthed at Trinity Bay. A telegraphic link had been established between the continents, to hook up the developing cable networks of Europe and North America.

At first, transatlantic contact was intermittent, highly expensive and agonisingly slow. Queen Victoria's ninety-eight-word message of congratulations to President

Buchanan on his election took sixteen hours to send in Morse code from London to Washington. The President's reply – after the US government had checked it was not being hoaxed – was marginally quicker: one hundred and forty-nine words in a mere ten hours.

During the first month four hundred messages passed across the Atlantic, including news of Britain's defeat in the Indian Mutiny.

Then, suddenly, the cable failed – victim of corrosion, faulty design and the use of incorrect voltages. It was another eight years before an improved new cable was laid. 'In 1865 they tried again, using the world's largest steam ship, Brunel's *Great Eastern*, a phenomenal piece of technology and the only one big enough to carry the weight, but the cable broke six hundred miles short of Newfoundland.' The following year she set off again, with the full two thousand miles of heavy cable crammed into her enormous hold, and steamed from Valentia to a different Newfoundland destination, the deep, sheltered bay at Heart's Content. 'As soon as they had landed the cable, the ship turned and went back to find the cable from the year before. Incredibly, they found it and splayed and spliced it together so that there were two working cables.' The *Great Eastern* cables were soon joined by others and, for a century, provided one of the chief methods of communication between the continents.

On 12 December 1901, Guglielmo Marconi placed a four-hundred-foot kite-supported antenna on Signal Hill to receive the first transatlantic wireless transmission, made from Poldhu in Cornwall. He heard the letter S tapped out in Morse code. 'It came through a little device called a coherer that changed the electro-magnetic waves into a sound wave but it wasn't like the well-modulated sounds we hear today. In Marconi's day, it was more like a lightning strike. They must have chosen S because in Morse it's nice and short and couldn't be mistaken for anything else. Of course, when the Titanic sank in 1912, only three hundred miles from here, Morse code and "SOS" saved many of the passengers.'

By 1920 the island was still achieving firsts, in the history of communications: one of the earliest transatlantic transmissions of the human voice took place between a room in the Cable Tower and the steam-ship Victoria, positioned just off the English coast. Today, the Society of Newfoundland Radio Amateurs operates a ham (amateur) radio station on the second floor of the tower.

∼ Standing Alone ∼

During the American Civil War relations between Britain and Canada were strained. A raid into Canada by Irish Americans to 'emancipate Ireland and also to annihilate England', was never likely to succeed, but it contributed to a Canadian sense of insecurity. Thousands of young Americans crossed the border to avoid conscription – more followed a hundred years later. British neutrality enraged some sections of the American press, who demanded an invasion of Canada. It was highly unlikely to happen but, even so, the British garrison was strengthened. Relations between the US and Canada took another knock in October 1864 when US northern forces pursued Confederate raiders into Canada and captured them. They handed them over to a Canadian magistrate, who promptly released them. At that time British North America consisted of Québec, the first French colony, and Ontario, with the vast wilderness of the North West Territories stretching from Labrador to British Columbia – named at the suggestion of Queen Victoria. In the east, the Maritime Provinces consisted of New Brunswick and Nova Scotia on the mainland, with Newfoundland and the tiny Prince Edward Island. Defence against potential US pressure made some further unity essential but agreement was difficult. The mainland colonies agreed to federate in the new Dominion – the word was chosen to avoid to upsetting the Americans – of Canada in 1868, but Prince Edward Island held out until 1875.

Newfoundland refused to consider federation. Apart from a spirit of independence there was an old argument over Labrador, where jurisdiction had gone to and fro between Newfoundland and Canada before finally, in 1809, ending up with Newfoundland. The dispute was only settled in 1949, when Newfoundland agreed to become part of the Dominion of Canada.

From the outside, Carla Clayton's house in the heart of St John's looks like many others in Newfoundland – picturesque weatherboard painted royal blue. Inside, though, we stepped back into the Victorian age. The hall was dark, and filled with a large collection of Victorian artefacts. Carla chairs the Newfoundland branch of the Monarchist League of Canada, whose members believe that the British monarchy has a vital role to play in contemporary Canadian society. She collects Victorian bits and other royal memorabilia including *Empire* magazine, royal annuals, guides to royalty and the empire that date from the fifties. Just about everything, from biscuit tins to mirrors, had come from Britain. Carla showed us into her sitting room, which was dedicated, as was the dining room, to her collections. Over tea and cake, we admired her china, photographs, tea caddies, lithographs, cabinets and, of course, Union flags. 'I've been interested in the monarchy since I was a young girl growing up in Nova Scotia,' she told us. 'I can remember going to my grandmother's house and seeing some of the pieces that are here.' Her oldest items are a 1788 King George III coin, which she wears as a necklace, and a 'white metal coronation piece of George IV', and the most recent include doll replicas of the royal family. Her fascination with monarchy is inspired by seeing the lives of kings and queens played out on a public stage and the conflict they face between private feelings and duty. She reminded us about George V's decision to put country before family and abandon his cousin Tsar Nicholas II during the Russian Revolution when he could have saved him and his family. 'How do you make those kind of decisions? You're a human being and you're the head of state, and this was a family member.'

How do other Newfoundlanders feel about their link with Britain? 'Some people feel that Newfoundland should have been a republic. That's why you sometimes see the pink, white and green flag here. The referendum to join Canada was won by a very small margin. But as I've only lived here for twenty-five years I don't have the right to have an attitude yet. I'm still thought of as someone from another part of Canada.'

∾ *The Great Fish War* ∾

Another reason why Newfoundlanders wanted to remain independent was that they feared the Canadian government would agree to the American demand for access to the island's fish. They hoped that Britain would stand firm against it. The arguments began after the 1812 war between Britain and the United States had ended. In the peace settlement of 1818 Britain conceded a number of rights to the Americans within Newfoundland waters, but others, regarded by some as essential, were excluded.

Newfoundland governments insisted on enforcing the letter of the law, which led to friction. Britain was concerned to maintain good relations with the United States but could do little but expostulate: like Jamaica, Newfoundland was one of those annoyingly independent colonies.

Newfoundlanders continued to irritate British governments by insisting on their rights to arrest American fishing-boats that infringed the agreements. In particular they objected to the use of seine nets, which swept up fish of all sizes, instead of the traditional purse nets, which were less efficient but preserved stocks. In 1910, after numerous investigations, conferences, delegations and bad-tempered correspondence, Britain took the dilemma to the international court at The Hague. As usual, the persistent Newfoundlanders won.

France was being difficult, too. After the Crimean War, in which Britain and France had acted as allies for the first time since the seventeenth century, the diplomats tried to clear up the status of the French shore. The Colonial Secretary, Henry Labouchere, who held office between 1855–8, agreed that the French should be given exclusive rights to the opposite coast of Labrador. Newfoundland saw this as a gross betrayal by their mother country, and talked of issuing a unilateral declaration of independence or of joining the United States. Labouchere was forced to withdraw the agreement and to promise never to make another without the consent of the Newfoundland government. In turn France was indignant, but nothing could be done. Commissioners were appointed and the debate continued.

That was when the lobster debate erupted. If lobsters were fish, they were French; if not, Newfoundlanders could catch them. In 1895, when France and Britain were on the brink of war in Africa, the French threatened to send a warship to Newfoundland. In 1904 a deal was done: in a typically imperial compromise, the British agreed not to interfere with the French invasion of Morocco if Newfoundland could keep its lobsters. The Great Fish War was won.

From the warmth of Carla's living room, we headed off to Tors Cove – for a beach party. Newfoundland's remoteness has meant that small communities have developed a strongly individual culture. The majority of settlers who migrated during the late eighteenth and early nineteenth centuries from south-west England or southern Ireland brought with them folk songs and ballads, ghost and fairy stories and traditional dances. While they are long forgotten back home, they remain a major focus of Newfoundland life. The ghost stories were often linked to the woods and the sea, both dangerous to newcomers.

We were about to experience Newfoundland hospitality

at a 'kettle party' when lobsters would be cooked in one large pot to the strains of traditional Irish music and folk stories. By the time we arrived, night had fallen and only a few had braved the weather to huddle under a tarpaulin beside a fire. As their children dammed a stream, jumping into the resulting deep puddles, the adults sang us a couple of Celtic-influenced songs when the rain eased off a little, but no one's heart was in it and, after a while, we all decided to call a halt. All, that is, except the children. As we drove away we watched them in the rear-view mirror, splashing about in the dim firelight and getting soaked.

Apparently, early settlers brought with them a belief in 'the good people' or 'the little people', supernatural beings in human form who lived in the woods or on the rocks by settlements, and stories of fairy mischief are rife across the island. The following day we travelled to Calvert, a three-hundred-year-old fishing village on the southern shore. There, we met Michael Walsh, a retired fisherman with a distinctive Irish accent, who lived with his wife just outside the town.

We followed him up a steep hill directly behind his house. The sky had cleared and, for the only time while we were in Newfoundland, the sun came out. We caught a breathtaking view of the harbour: the water was a glorious deep-blue complemented by the ochre grass. The higher we climbed, the more of the coast we could see. At the mouth of the wide harbour a single huge rock formed a solitary island, mist curling round its summit.

At the top of the hill the meadow gave way to conifer forest. Michael gazed into the trees from a safe distance. Fifty paces further on, we would be in the haunt of the

JAMAICA

Idyllic Jamaica.

Talking to James about the pirate stronghold at Port Royal, Jamaica.

Freddie McGregor who tried to explain the African roots of reggae – I couldn't really get it. But he gave me a nice mango.

The Bruckins Dancers from Zion Hill Primary School – behind the camera are, of course, all their mums!

Lovers' Leap –
where, allegedly, the
slave lovers jumped
to their death rather
than be parted. They
must have been very
good at jumping to
avoid those bushes.

Crocodile hunting on Black River.
Found one.

Colonel Sydney Peddie in Accompong, Jamaica – back in the rain forest after 30 years in Tooting.

All these ladies had mobile phones attached to their belts. We filmed them – they filmed us.

This is the camoflage the escaped slaves, the Maroons, wore to wage guerrilla war on the British.

The Kindah Tree, where leaders of the escaped tribes met to make peace and decide to unite to fight the British. They shared rum mixed with the blood of each tribe and declared themselves Kindah (One Family).

Fairfield Great House just outside Montego Bay. One of Jamaica's grand plantation houses.

NEWFOUNDLAND

Cabot's Tower, St. John's, Newfoundland, partly shrouded in mist. Which was unusual. It was usually completely shrouded in fog.

Charlie Conway, whose house is a living museum of her love of and loyalty to our Royal Family.

This is Michael Walsh. This man believes in fairies. I don't.

The rugged scenery of Newfoundland's Southern Shore shows the harsh winters that new settlers would have had to endure.

A canine statue shows the union of two of Canada's territories, Newfoundland and Labrador.

This is me hiding from two ladies who are trying to make me eat Olde Worlde English food.

fairies. Michael always carried a little piece of bread in his pocket. Why? 'The fairies are supposed to be about a foot-and-a-half tall, part English and part Irish. If you go into the wood without a bit of bread in your pocket, ten chances to one they'll get you. It's never happened to me, thanks be to God, but a man from round here was once warned not to go into the wood without a piece of bread. "Come on," he said. "There's no fairies." He laughed and went in on his own. He didn't come out. When his friend found him, he was about half a mile in and had fallen asleep. His boots and coat were missing. It sounds like the fairies mugged him. There are lots of stories like that. My mother would never let me go into the woods without a piece of bread, and if I forgot it, I'd race back down the road at forty kilometres an hour.'

Folklorists have discovered that these stories date back to the nineteenth century and earlier, having been passed down the generations. When Michael was a boy there was little communication with the outside world, so fairy stories were the mainstay of an evening's entertainment. Michael had given us a brief insight into what the early settlers would have talked about, how they kept them-selves entertained and the strong sense they had that they were still Irish and Cornish, even though they had left their homeland.

Their isolation from the rest of the world meant that their speech patterns were preserved. Linguists visit the island to study the spoken language, which, in some areas, is thought to be the purest form of Elizabethan English still used. Some people still say 'ye' rather than 'you', and others have Irish accents.

Our last call was on the Avalon peninsula where we saw the vast archaeological excavation of the Colony of Avalon. The English explorer, Sir George Calvert founded the community at Ferryland in 1621. He sent a Welshman, Captain Edward Wainover, with eleven settlers as an advance party. Once the colony was established, Calvert went out to settle there himself, but by 1629 he had abandoned it for Chesapeake because of the weather, leaving thirty settlers behind. We sympathised.

Ferryland remains a small coastal community that depended originally on fishing, farming and trade. The archaeological dig there has turned up thousands of artefacts, giving clues to the early colonists' way of life. An Interpretive Center tells their story, and it was there that we met Sheila Roberts. In seventeenth-century costume of white blouse, black bodice, red skirt, white apron and cap, she took us into a replica seventeenth-century kitchen where she introduced us to the diet of those early settlers, which included barley broth – 'a favourite with the seamen' – tansy omelette, cabbage potage and preserved fruit. 'The settlers brought with them supplies including grain, livestock, spices, sugar and butter. They traded fish with the southern European countries for olive oil, wine, spices, raisins and almonds. They cooked everything with white wine because at first they were suspicious of the water because in England it was very polluted. They would have lived quite well.'

Once the settlers had finished the supplies they had brought with them, their diet changed: 'There are different sorts of edible roots here as well as raspberries, blueberries, bake apples, and partridge berries, which grew wild on the island. They would have incorporated them into their diet. They always cooked fruit, making pies but particularly preserves and jams. They ate seasonally, so during the summer they'd have dishes that used cream, then come the fall they'd kill some animals – it was too expensive to keep them all through the winter – then pickle the meat and salt the fish.' In spring, Sheila went on, 'They describe the kitchen garden here as having all sorts of turnip, cabbage, carrots, parsnips and radishes as big as a man's arm. They grew herbs for medicine and cooking.' The land wasn't as fertile as it had been back home, but the settlers compensated for that with back-breaking work. Fish, principally cod, was a mainstay of their diet.

Towards the end of the nineteenth century, at the height of Empire, most of the men on the island were employed in fish-related businesses, and up to ninety per cent of exports were fish products. Today, overfishing has virtually wiped out the cod. We have come a long way from the days when John Cabot could write that 'The sea is full of fish, which are not only taken with a net, but also with a basket.'

~ *A Tailpiece* ~

Nineteenth-century Newfoundland was best known for its superb dogs. A gentle breed, with webbed feet, they are powerful swimmers and natural rescue dogs (champion Newfoundlands must be able to tow a boat and bring a human swimmer to shore). Fishing schooners habitually carried a Newfoundland as the ship's dog. In 1919 the whole company of a stranded steam-ship was saved by the ship's dog, which carried a line to shore.

Newfoundland dogs were popular on both sides of the Atlantic

Queen Victoria admired them at a distance. She preferred small dogs, the King Charles spaniels, the Pekinese and the Italian greyhound among her favourites. The Prince of Wales, however, had a Newfoundland, and in 1901 the island's prime minister gave one to the future King George V to amuse his children.

The most enduringly famous specimen of the breed must be the 'prim Newfoundland dog called Nana', who looked after the Darling children in J. M. Barrie's *Peter Pan*.

Our overwhelming impression of Newfoundland was of its isolation, but that might have had more to do with the fog than its geographical location. The people were warm and welcoming and, when the fog lifted, the beauty of the landscape was well worth the wait.

With so many towns and villages focused on the sea and the living it offered, we were all too aware of the tragedy caused by centuries of over-whaling and over-fishing. Fishing people have lived there for generations in an endless struggle with the elements for the sea's bounty, but no longer.

4

India

Our next trip was in August, not the ideal time you might think, to be strolling round Calcutta. But luckily I'd just been in Barrow-in-Furness filming, and I'd spent a lot of time on a beach in forty-degree heat, in a hat, tweed coat and a wig, so Calcutta actually felt quite refreshing. We then flew to Delhi, and changed planes to Bogdagra, which is in the foothills of the Himalayas. We had the most spectacular three-hour drive, going up and up into the mountains. Along the road we passed schoolchildren on their way home. They were in very smart uniforms, really well turned out, and they had beautiful colouring, brown faces with lovely pink cheeks. And lots of the girls had plaits tied with ribbons. All very different from the dear old pasty-faced hoop-earringed gum-chewers in ballet flats we're used to at home.

We stopped half-way up at a café for a cup of tea – a little shack on a sort of shelf hanging over the tea terraces. I couldn't see any laughing ladies in saris plucking shoots and popping them into a basket, but I thought perhaps that was just on the packets and doesn't actually happen. It would be a bit like expecting our harvests to be gathered in by girls clutching individual sheaves, like the Ovaltine advert by the train line.

Our hotel in Darjeeling was called the Windamere. Oh dear – should I mention the spelling at reception? I wondered. The lounge bookcase was full of yellowed Agatha Christie paperbacks, and the whole hotel was like the setting for one. My room had a musty dark red patterned carpet, an ancient claw-foot bathtub, and the sort of wonky electric fire you normally only see in stately homes or in a 'How We Used To Live' exhibition at the Science Museum. The restaurant offered a four-course set meal – and, hedging its bets cuisine-wise, had as the second course curry, followed by meat and two veg. The music playing in the background was a British wartime favourite, the crooner Al Bowlly, whom we had just used in *Housewife, 49*. I hadn't expected to hear him again so soon, or so high up.

The next morning we filmed on what they call affectionately the Toy Train – only the second railway in the world to become a World Heritage Site. It was designed by an Englishman who worked for the East Bengal Railway. It used to take the English memsahibs three days to get from the heat of Calcutta to the cool of the Darjeeling hill station, but this feat of engineering cut the time to a matter of hours.

It's a steam train, two-foot gauge, not particularly charming inside, a bit like the carriage of a 1960s diesel train, but it chuffs right up the middle of the village streets once a day, as the local people wave and bat bits of cinder out of their hair. The gradient is so steep, you really feel the engine struggle; it makes you want to get out and push, but it copes, it gets there. It was a novelty, though, to be wandering up a village street and see a train coming up right behind you.

∽ *Introduction* ∽

In the early seventeenth century, British merchants came to India seeking the Mughal emperor's permission to trade. A century later they dominated the scene, and by the 1760s the British East India Company had become the foremost Indian power. Brilliant leadership and effective discipline enabled the Company's forces to defeat much larger Indian armies, but rapid territorial expansion and the introduction of new ideas led to the Indian Mutiny of 1856. In 1858 the British government took direct control, with Queen Victoria later styled Empress of India, and British-appointed administrators governing the sub-continent. The British Raj transformed not only India but Britain, and encouraged the development of democratic Indian nationalism. Independent since 1947, and a republic within the Commonwealth since 1950, India is today the world's largest democracy.

When we announced we were going to Calcutta, or Kolkata, many people reacted with sympathy. When we added that we would be visiting during the monsoon, they were horrified, and regaled us with stories about malarial mosquitoes, streets flowing with tidal waves of sewage, the distressing poverty and filth. We left Newfoundland with our hearts in our boots.

Out of all India, we had chosen to begin with Calcutta because it was the capital of British India between 1772 and 1912, the showpiece of the Raj and the jewel in the empire's crown. During the summer, the city's British residents would send their wives and children to the cooler hill station of Darjeeling, so we had decided to make it our second port of call. We set out to discover how the British had come to be there, how they lived and the impact they made on India and on themselves.

Calcutta, like so many Indian cities, bombards the senses. The streets are a torrent of cars and people: open-air food stalls, street traders touting for business, rickshaws running in and out of the traffic, beggars, holy men, businesspeople, nuns and schoolchildren. Billboards stand one in front of another; houses and other dwellings are jammed tightly together, and shops are stuffed with goods piled higgledy-piggledy high. Everywhere frantic hooting accompanies the roar of engines – on the back of virtually every vehicle a sign reads 'Horn Please'. The colours were intense, with exquisite combinations of turquoise, orange and yellow that had faded in the rain. All this was overlaid with the smell of woodfires, cooking and incense.

Bright yellow Ambassador taxis fought for space as they wove past faded portraits of Mother Teresa and small makeshift roadside shrines. Although banned from the city now, the odd cow still holds up the traffic as police in spotless uniforms stand on precarious podiums to bring order to the rush-hour. Pollution hangs heavy over the city, and in the evening it turns Calcutta a glorious pink, the sun's last rays caught in the thick air. In torrential monsoon rain the city comes to a standstill: there is no sign of road rage, just patience.

An even more vivid world exists in the side-streets: on street corners men bathe at standpipes while stall-holders stir fry or toss the ingredients for snacks, the air thick with ginger and spices. Groups of women glide about, giggling, their thick black hair shiny, their saris vibrant – hot pink and red, acid lime and sapphire, aquamarine and orange. In a darker corner a man with distorted feet and cloudy eyes looks up blindly from the ground, sensing human presence. A woman and her child lie sleeping under a makeshift shelter – just two of the many who live on the streets.

As it turned out, the dire warnings we had received proved wrong. The monsoon rain was warm – no worse than an autumnal downpour in Surrey, and never resulted in a flood of raw sewage. The mosquitoes (malarial or not) kept a respectful distance and we were never aware of anything filthier or smellier than you'd experience on a brisk walk through anywhere in Britain.

∼ *The East India Company* ∼

In 1606 Dutch ships annihilated a Spanish fleet off Malacca. Nine years later the British defeated the Portuguese near Goa. 'Most of their vessels were destroyed by the British,' the Mughal emperor Jahangir wrote in his memoirs, the first mention of the British in any Mughal record. It signified the decline in India of the Iberian powers and the rise of the British.

Shah Jahangir, who ruled an empire that stretched from Afghanistan to Burma and (sometimes shakily) over all India, could not take the pretensions of the impoverished British too seriously, but in 1616 he enjoyed the visit of the first accredited ambassador, Sir Thomas Roe, to his court. The two men travelled and drank together, 'with many passages of jests, mirth and bragges . . .' The Emperor was 'very merry and joyful, and cracked like a Northern man'.

Sir Thomas's journey was financed by the English East India Company, established in 1600 by a group of London merchants who proposed, rather vaguely, a voyage '. . . to the Est Indies and other islandes and cuntries thereabouts . . .'. Sir Thomas's persistent socialising eventually persuaded the emperor to offer his protection to the little British station at Surat, on the west coast; thereafter British merchants concentrated on India, and left the eastern islands to the Dutch.

As the new trade flourished, India's influence on Britain made itself felt: cheap cotton fabric meant that underclothes became readily available, with a notable improvement in personal hygiene, and the China tea that the Company's ships imported began to oust beer as the breakfast drink.

～ Calcutta ～

The Dutch had spotted the advantages of a trading station on the delta of the river Ganges, which leads into the heart of northern India, and built a factory on the Hooghly, a branch of the Ganges, in the 1620s. By the end of the century, the nearby British settlement at Fort William had overtaken its rivals, and in 1717, when the Mughal Emperor granted the East India Company freedom to trade throughout Bengal, Orissa and Bihar, the town of Calcutta began to expand. Those provinces were, by some way, the most advanced, industrially and commercially, in India, and the splendid fabrics their weavers produced transformed European fashion. Attracted by the security of British rule, local people flocked to share in the commercial benefits:

Calcutta in the 1830s

Indian intermediaries negotiated contracts and Bengali bankers provided funding for British ventures. The other two centres of British influence, Madras and Bombay, reluctantly yielded precedence to the Calcutta Presidency.

Originally a trade settlement established by the East India Trading Company, Calcutta was built along the banks of the river Hooghly. We wanted to observe the city from the water, so one early morning we took a boat from a pontoon that sported a fantastic rusty old 'Police' sign – an art director couldn't have designed it better. Further along the river at the ferry jetty, men with briefcases stood patiently against peeling railings and others squatted on their haunches, all waiting to go to work.

We journeyed up the muddy brown waters of the huge river, with all its commercial traffic, as offerings of flowers floated by. We saw people bathing and washing clothes on the *ghats* (steps) that lead down to the water. We passed an eclectic mix of buildings – grand structures that had been centres of commerce in Calcutta's heyday, a tower with a tree growing through its roof, and temples. It felt a little voyeuristic to watch the everyday routines of washing and praying, but no one seemed bothered by our presence as they poured water over their heads. Then we spotted a line of bare backsides crouched over the river . . . !

Back on the shore, we went to look at one of the *ghats* that line the Hooghly's banks where hundreds of men were washing – toothbrushes and bars of soap lay on the shallow steps. They also rinsed their *dhotis*, then put them on wet, ready to start the day's work. We soon pulled a crowd, but others continued to wash and pray. As we started to film, we asked a particularly enthusiastic chanter, an elderly white-bearded man, to quieten down. He ignored us, as did his fellows, while our sound recordist looked on in mild concern. Then we were told that he was a holy man, leading the prayers, and we were interrupting a religious ritual.

We sat down on the steps, with Toby Sinclair, an amateur historian, hoping he would tell us something about India as it once was and as it is today. A tall, well-built bearded Scotsman in his fifties, he is married to an Indian and has lived in India for more than thirty years. As we talked, we were reassured to see the small dark sweat patch on Toby's light-blue shirt expanding. Even a naturalised local was feeling the humidity. First he explained what was happening on the *ghat*: 'The Hooghly is one of the arms of the Ganges so it's a sacred river. These people go to the water for three reasons: one is to cleanse themselves spiritually; another is to cleanse themselves physically, which you might wonder at, given the detritus in the water; lastly, it's a social gathering where people come to meet and chant. Many of the ghats were developed and sponsored by landlords, who made their wealth in the seventeenth and eighteenth centuries, and the maharajahs. Some, like this one, are exclusively for men, others for women.'

How and why had the British arrived in Calcutta in 1690? 'The Dutch were already established here and controlled many parts of the Indian trade. Initially the English East India Company came to trade too, sailing up the Hooghly towards the heartland of northern India. They traded in textiles, particularly silk and cotton, then later in indigo. There were huge indigo plantations up-river, run with indentured labour – a little-talked-about dark side of English history in India. They also traded opium, which was grown upstream, and saltpetre, a key ingredient in gunpowder. As the trade expanded into India, the English East India Company needed to patrol their sources of supply. Their charter allowed them to raise a force to protect themselves as they expanded. It developed into a private army that operated throughout India. Initially we were welcomed, but later we tried to take control and that caused resentment.'

∾ The Black Hole of Calcutta ∾

The door behind the pillars is thought to lead to the Black Hole

In 1707, after the death of the Emperor Aurangzeb, Mughal rule began to disintegrate, with French, English and ambitious Indians struggling for ascendancy. Calcutta's prosperity offered a tempting target for the Muslim Governor Nawab Siraj-ud-Daula, who successfully attacked the settlement in July 1756. Sixty of his prisoners were crammed into a tiny cell, where most suffocated overnight. The infamous 'Black Hole of Calcutta' fuelled British indignation and gave Colonel Robert Clive the opportunity to impose British hegemony on India. Clive was avaricious and unbalanced but a military genius. He made a secret agreement with a rival Nawab and the Bengali Jaged Seth banking family, which in 1757, coupled with his own able leadership and the fighting qualities of his mainly Indian soldiers, enabled his tiny force to defeat twenty times its number at the decisive battle of Plassey. Siraj-ud-Daula was murdered by his rival Mir Jafir, and Clive became Governor General of Bengal. In 1765, when the dust had settled, the Emperor Shah Alam, hoping for Clive's help in his war against the rebellious Marathas, granted the East India Company the perpetual title of Diwan – Treasurer – of Bengal, Bihar and Orissa.

The Company agreed to pay Shah Alam about £250,000 annually, and in return took control of the richest provinces of India. It was to govern, ostensibly on the Emperor's behalf, 'agreeably to the rule of Mahomet and the laws of the [Mughal] Empire'.

Robert Clive at the Battle of Plassey

The climate must have been a rude shock to those Englishmen who came to India. Toby told us that their average life expectancy was two monsoons, until they adapted to the climate, adopting Indian clothes and abandoning game pie in favour of Indian food. 'They started at six in the morning and worked through to noon,' he explained. 'Then they'd have a meal, before resting until four or five in the afternoon when they went back to work. Some took Indian mistresses, who were often referred to as "sleeping dictionaries" – the British learnt the language of the country from the women they slept with. Those white men became the nouveaux riches of the eighteenth century. When they went home they found themselves richer than the British aristocracy.'

～ To Protect and Cherish the Inhabitants ～

Once firmly established in Bengal, British governments had to decide what to do about India. The East India Company's profits and the duty charged on Indian imports provided an important source of revenue. The London directors rarely had a chance to settle on a policy for the Company, thanks to the slowness of communications – a round voyage lasted at least six months – and to the ambitious initiatives of the 'men on the spot', which pushed events along.

The men on the spot could plunder Indian resources almost unchecked until the trial of Warren Hastings, who was accused of misgovernment and corruption. The India Act of 1784 put a stop to that sort of thing by implementing the rule of law in Indian affairs. It was, the Company and the British government agreed, morally and commercially necessary to 'protect and cherish the inhabitants whose interest and welfare are now become our primary care'.

The number of those 'inhabitants' increased remarkably quickly. By the end of the Napoleonic Wars the Company controlled almost all of the Ganges valley, the whole of the east coast, and much of the west. The Court of Directors 'cherished' an empire, marshalled huge armies – they could put a hundred thousand men in the field – and sold tea. Even for pragmatic British governments this was absurd, and in 1833 the Company was instructed to abandon its trade and concentrate on running India, where the population under British control was then probably about a hundred million. Company rule was underpinned by some twenty thousand British soldiers, supported by Indian recruits, but to be successful it needed the Indians' consent and co-operation. Popularity was not essential, which was just as well: many of the rulers lacked any understanding of Indian sensitivities.

By now we were forming an idea of the scale of the British operation in India. The country was unquestionably the jewel in Britain's crown, with wealth enjoyed by both British and Indians, who built houses that reflected their wealth and power. As Western architecture became fashionable, so British architects found work in Calcutta. Some of these lavish buildings have survived and been well maintained, but others have crumbled.

The extraordinary Marble Palace was built in 1835 and now houses a collection of art. The Mullick Bari at Pathuriaghata was built by Raja Rajendra Mullick. The house fronts on to a busy side-street, and stands in a small, overgrown garden behind rusted railings. The entrance lies on the other side of a brick archway, past rusty old cars and a statue of an angel.

We went through a heavy wooden door and found ourselves in a square courtyard, with raised pillared walkways along which stood marble busts, wooden furniture and faded photographs. But the central courtyard, with paved floor and intricate free-standing cast-ironwork, bright green with age, was striking. The ironwork had been brought from Britain at the height of the Industrial Revolution but had been designed by British architects to replicate the traditional courtyard of a Bengali home. For many years the iron left over from the job had been stored in the mansion's basement.

We were fortunate that Rajat Mullick was available to show us round. The house had been built by his great-great-great-great-grandfather more than a hundred and fifty years ago. 'At that time,' Rajat began, 'British architects reigned supreme over the urban architecture of Calcutta. The person who designed this house was British because there was no qualified Indian to build such a place then. It was fashionable to have a palatial building so people thought you were a nobleman and you could host functions, like parties, dances and puja [worship], that today go on in public places.'

He was reticent about his family's wealth, which had derived from their association with the East India Company. 'My grandfather's grandfather's grandfather was a banker for them and indirectly helped the British. That was his business then.' He also mentioned the spiritual significance of the house, which had been visited in

1883 by the great Indian philosopher and religious leader Sri Ramakrishna. 'He had spontaneous transcendental meditation and he was unconscious,' Mr Mullick explained. 'But he didn't lie down. He was almost unconscious, sitting in a yoga position. This is why our house is historically important and where we are focused.'

∼ *Friendly Relations* ∼

Earlier British arrivals had soon accepted Indian customs, slipping easily into pajamas, smoking nargilas and acquiring a taste for Indian cooking. Colonel Hercules Skinner, who died in 1803, married a Rajput noblewoman; his son James, born in 1778, and said to have had fourteen wives, formed

A trooper of Skinner's Horse

the famous cavalry corps 'Skinner's Horse', also known as the 'Yellow Boys', who wore traditional Rajput robes and remain one of the most distinguished regiments of the Indian Army.

Colonel Mordaunt matched his fighting cocks against those of the Nawab of Awadh, and the diarist William Hickey, who spent a riotous time in Calcutta in the 1770s, was deeply attached to his mistress, Jemdanee, who bore him a son. But when the new century dawned and Englishwomen, the 'memsahibs', arrived, outward propriety had to be maintained, and discretion observed.

After only a few days in India, we had noticed that the people of Calcutta seemed much more laid-back than we Westerners. Was the tolerant atmosphere typical of India? 'That is true,' said Rajat, 'because India is multicultural. There's no Indian "race". We are Bengali, but the next state is Bihar, whose language and culture are different. We survive by being tolerant of others and their different points of view.'

Did he think it was a good or bad thing that Indians seem so easily to have absorbed the British Empire? 'There is no unique answer to that,' he replied. 'We have a long history of being under somebody. Before the British we were under the Mughals. It was just different when the British were here. First they came as traders but then, after making money, they wanted to reign over the whole country.' He felt that their presence had been positive and negative. 'A bad aspect of the missionaries was that they wanted to convert Hindus into Christians. A good aspect was that they set up educational institutions and hospitals, and looked after the poor and downtrodden. Everything has a good and bad aspect. There are world-class educational institutions in India now, which were set up by British missionaries. I also think the British taught us to value our heritage. Even the freedom struggle [which resulted in Indian independence in 1947] was a result of British education. The leaders were educated in Britain. Their eyes were opened, and that is what freedom means.'

~ Peace, Order and the Rule of Law ~

The British Raj transformed India, but India permanently changed its rulers. Successive British governments had been reluctant imperialists: colonies were a nuisance, likely to be expensive, and best accorded self-government as soon as possible. In fact, few other European countries were as poorly equipped to run a great empire as Britain. British law was incoherent and outdated – trial by battle was abolished as late as the 1820s – and there was no police service until 1827. Local and regional government were still in the hands of medieval corporations and lords lieutenant. Education was largely irrelevant at a time when France and Germany both had well-designed national systems. The army was small and unprofessional: commissions were bought and sold. The only two first-class organisations were the Royal Navy and the City of London, the twin pillars that supported the British Empire.

India could not be governed by such a muddled system. To some extent the East India Company had accepted this by establishing civil and military colleges to train competent soldiers and administrators. After the assumption of direct rule the new 'public' schools trained great numbers of officers for the imperial and colonial services.

The Indian Civil Service, which Rudyard Kipling described as 'the first fighting line' of imperial rule, became a byword for thorough and incorruptible administration of a quality never seen before in either India or Britain. Its recruits were selected after they had sat a series of stiff examinations. Under its aegis, India was brought into the world economy. The ICS enjoyed the highest-possible credit rating, so it succeeded in raising loans in London and in India. Communications were built to a standard unparalleled elsewhere in Asia: by the end of the nineteenth century India had twenty-four thousand miles of railway compared to China's three hundred and forty. Traditional industries such as metal-work and cotton-spinning declined, affected by the industrial revolution, but the Indian cotton industry was now one of the world's largest.

Indian political institutions were slow to develop. Although it was accepted that, sooner or later, Indians must govern themselves, the British regarded that as, at best, a distant prospect. Britain's responsibility was to 'establish peace, order and the supremacy of law, the prevention of crime, the redress of wrong, and enforcement of contracts . . . [and] the construction of public works'. India was a concept, a tradition, the ancient land of Hind, rather than a political entity, divided as it was among many races and religions, and even more languages. But the new social fabric, with schools, colleges and a thriving

vernacular press, ensured that a concept of Indian nationality emerged. With it came the demand for Indian
self-government.

It was a wrench to leave Rajat Mullik's splendid house,
but we were curious to find out how the British had
lived when they arrived in India. In the plush surround-
ings of the Saturday Club bar, we met up with
Rudrangshu Mukherjee, an author and academic, who
now edits the *Calcutta Telegraph*. We began by asking him
how the British in India had become so wealthy. 'Largely
through trade, but looting and plundering was an
important aspect of it too. In 1717, the then Mughal
emperor gave the English East India Company special
permission to trade in India duty free but the servants of
the Company began to use that special privilege to service their own interests, claiming there was no distinction
between the private trade of the Company's servants and
the Company's trade. After the 1757 battle of Plassey,
the British became the political masters of Bengal and
had a free run. The fortunes made in Bengal from trade,
coercion and plunder were fantastic. Some Bengalis
became partners of the British when they began trading
and received commission on the trade; they built many
of the big mansions in Calcutta. There was a lot of
mutual benefit to be had.' During this period, the
phrase 'shaking the pagoda tree' (a pagoda was an
Indian coin) was adopted to reflect the sizeable profits
that could be made.

When the British emerged as the élite of Calcutta, most

of them lived in the area around Park Street and Dalhousie Square, which became known as 'White Town'. 'There were long tree-lined avenues and houses,' Rudrangshu went on, 'built in European style, with gardens and beautiful manicured lawns, modelled on the mansions of nineteenth-century Britain.' During the second half of the eighteenth century, the British mixed with Calcutta society. 'We have descriptions of parties given by rich Bengalis to which the British were also invited. We have accounts of how the British in Calcutta adapted to some of the Indian customs. Then the British women came to look for husbands – the "fishing fleet", they were called – and segregation began to take place. By the 1820s or 1830s, I would say that it was complete.'

The arrival of William Bentinck as governor general in 1828 prompted the British to assert their moral superiority over the Indians. 'He set out an agenda to reform Indian society,' Rudrangshu explained. 'Certain Indian institutions were identified as "barbaric" – for example, the traditional custom of *sati*, which was particularly observed among middle-class Hindus, where a widow would burn herself on her husband's funeral pyre. He also began a series of educational reforms to teach Indian kids what was being taught in English public schools and at Oxbridge, regardless of their own local customs and culture. So, medical colleges were set up and, horror of horrors, the first dissection of a corpse took place.' Rudrangshu had to explain why this caused such uproar. 'In India you touched only the body of your own kin. You wouldn't touch the body of someone from a lower caste because that spoils your own.' And they didn't stop there.

'Western-trained doctors went inside Bengali houses to treat the women, and so broke down the system that kept women segregated and not allow them to come out in public. In 1855, a group of Bengalis put forward an initiative, which was supported and taken forward by the British governor, that would allow widows to remarry. Before that they were either on the funeral pyre or they led lives of poverty, rejected by their family.'

As the British became politically dominant, they annexed parts of northern India, removing rulers and changing established land and economic systems. 'A cherished world was disappearing very fast under the impact of British rule so there was a "churning" in Indian society as it encountered alien ideas. In 1857, it erupted into what the British call the Indian Mutiny and we call the Great Revolt.' The introduction of the Enfield rifle had sparked the uprising, Rudrangshu told us. The sepoys, soldiers, had to bite each cartridge so that they could pour the gunpowder into the barrel. 'A rumour went round that the grease on the cartridge was produced from pig and cow fat so the Muslim and Hindi sepoys refused to bite them for fear of spoiling their caste. The British officers refused to listen to their anxieties, which were transmitted to the villages. Eventually two regiments of the Bengal Army mutinied in Meerut, a little to the north-west of Delhi. But the interesting thing is that the civil population of peasantry, artisans, landlords and princes joined them, so the mutiny became an uprising. By the end of June, the British in the north-west of India had either been killed or had lost control. Lord Canning, the governor general, diverted British troops from China to north India. Within eight months, after a tremendous amount of violence, they had quelled the uprising.'

∽ Mutiny, or War of Independence? ∽

Emily Eden, the sister of Governor General Lord Auckland and a perceptive observer of Indian life in the 1840s, wrote, 'Given the thinness of the crust over the volcano on which we all sit in this country, the wonder is that it does not explode oftener.' The eruption came with the 'Indian Mutiny' in 1857, a turning-point in British and Indian

Indian sepoys defending Delhi against the British

history. It was much more than a military mutiny: Indian school text books refer to it as the First National War of Independence, which is almost as misleading since the violence was suppressed by British and Indian troops; but the effects of the passionate, conservative reaction to the imposition of new ideas were permanent. Despite warnings, such as Emily Eden's, the British were unprepared.

For the first time in the two hundred years since the English civil war, British civilians were caught up in extreme violence and the public were horrified. The aftermath of massacres at the Cawnpore Bibighar in which women and children were butchered, then thrown down a well, was chillingly recorded for all to see by the new photography. Painters, too, made dramatic representations of the actions that were eagerly received. At least one was thought too shocking and had to be altered: evil mutineers advancing on terrified women were replaced with brave Highlanders. With the help of the Sikhs and Gurkhas, both recent enemies of the British but now allies (more than four-fifths of the soldiers killed in the principal battle were Indian allies), the mutiny was crushed. The ring-leaders were executed by the old Mughal method: they were blown from the mouths of cannons. There were arguments both for clemency and for revenge but all agreed that a new order was essential.

Rudrangshu reminded us that the violence hadn't been one-sided: 'Any white man, woman or child they found they killed. They said it was a war against the *firenghi* [foreigners] who were out to destroy their religion.'

As a consequence of the mutiny, the British government

realised it was no longer possible to run India through the English East India Company and decided to take over. In 1877 it declared Queen Victoria to be Queen Empress of India. 'The irony is that yesterday's friends became tomorrow's enemies,' Rudrangshu observed wryly. 'Their Western education gave the people of India the tools to challenge the premise of British rule. Having learned the virtues of democracy, Indians wanted it for themselves. That is where the roots of Indian nationalism lie.'

∽ A New Era ∽

One sign of social change in nineteenth-century India was the establishment of printing presses, hitherto unknown in India, which sprung up everywhere. Between 1810 and 1820, no fewer than fifteen thousand books were printed in Bengali, mainly by Indian-owned presses. They stimulated discussion as people considered the potential merits of change, and talked about Utilitarianism, liberal democracy, Darwinism and socialism, and how they might apply to current Indian politics. If parliamentary democracy was the most perfect form of government, why should it not apply in India, as it did in other British territories, such as Canada, Australia and South Africa? The attempt to find an answer to this question occupied the British government for the next century.

With a clearer picture now of the British in India, we caught the narrow-gauge 'Toy Train' to Darjeeling, following the route of the families who once summered there.

The track is a phenomenal piece of engineering, which zigzags and loops beside the road through the villages and passes within a foot or two of ramshackle houses and shops. As the train chugs along, specks of hot ash float out of the billowing funnel to land on everyone and everything. If the window is open the ash is sucked into the carriage.

On the way up into the Himalayan foothills we passed through towns and villages bristling with activity, children marching to school in neat uniforms, books tucked under their arms.

Soon we were above the clouds, looking down into lush green valleys over houses clustered on hillsides. Prayer flags fluttered from the trees and from innumerable shrines as we travelled through terraced tea plantations where the pickers made their way along tightly packed rows of long bushes.

The higher we went, the cooler the atmosphere became, and when we arrived at Darjeeling station clouds shrouded the nearby hills. The town straddles a steep hill, with tight stairways squeezed between houses where pedestrians can cut through from one street to a higher or lower one. Up here, 4x4s negotiate the tortuous winding roads, although the centre of the town is closed to traffic. Now the weather had all the hallmarks of a British autumn: it was cold and rain alternated abruptly with clear skies and blazing heat.

The name 'Darjeeling' is a corruption of 'Dorje Ling', or 'Place of the Thunderbolt'. It is a thriving, colourful town, with magnificent views of the Himalayas and the majestic peak of Kanchenjunga, the third highest mountain in the world. Originally, the British came here for the sake of their health, but Darjeeling soon became a popular summer resort, whose reputation attracted socialites and adventurers.

~ Tea and Opium ~

By the mid-nineteenth century the British were consuming some £3 million worth, at wholesale prices, of China tea, and the British government collected twice that amount in

A tea plantation in Begal

duty. It was grown in China, shipped to India, where it was paid for in Indian opium, and re-exported to Britain.

Then in 1840 the Assam Tea Company began to experiment with local production. A few years later the eminent botanist Sir Joseph Hooker was kidnapped by the Rajah of Sikkim, and took the opportunity to study the area. He concluded that its climate, a thousand feet up in the foothills of the Himalayas, was eminently suitable for tea. Darjeeling was no longer just a hospital town: it expanded rapidly as the teas it produced became known and sought-after – first-flush Darjeeling is greatly prized – fetching high prices in the London market.

Major Kesang Lama, who had served with the British Gurkha Regiment, lives in the village of Ghoom, close to Darjeeling. The easiest way to get there is by the hill railway that runs through the heart of the little town. Ghoom sits at the highest point of the railway, an outcrop of tightly packed houses, linked with steep, narrow streets and balconies overlooking the Himalayan foothills. Every now and then we glimpsed bright green countryside down alleys that cut between tall, ramshackle buildings.

Major Lama's home was a first-floor apartment in a building on the side of a steep slope that headed down into tea plantation. We went into his living room, past a small curved wooden bar with highly polished glasses. It was filled with carvings, wooden statues and army mementoes. The major was perhaps in his early eighties but looked younger.

He and his wife gave us tea and cheese straws, and as

we watched the sun set through the room's long picture window, he talked about his army career. 'I was really keen to join the army because when I was in school our geography teacher used to tell us every time he entered the classroom, "The sun never sets on the British Empire." "Pardon, sir," I said, "what does the empire look like? Is it a small country or a big one?" And he said, "When you go to the army, you will find out what it is." So I wanted to see it from that time on.'

After Partition in 1947, an agreement between Nepal, India and Britain resulted in the transfer of four Gurkha regiments from the Indian Army to the British Army, where they eventually became the Gurkha Brigade. The soldiers had to choose between the British or the Indian Army. 'Then I said, "Now what am I to do?",' Major Lama recalled. 'My heart tells me, "Don't go to the British Army, you stay back in India." But my brain says, "No, no, no. Don't you like to see the British Empire? Jump over to the Union Jack and sign your name there. Your life will be better if you join the British Army. You will get better pay, better rations, better welfare."'

He trained as a wireless operator, then joined the 2nd Battalion, the Gurkha Rifles, and travelled the world, serving in Hong Kong, Malaya, Singapore, eastern Nepal, Egypt, Europe and England. 'So I am very grateful to the British Army. I had a chance to visit all these nice countries, nice men, different cultures.'

Later, back in Darjeeling, we called at the Planters' Club, which had a breathtaking view of the surrounding mountains and valleys and was once a was social hub for the British based in and around Darjeeling. There, we were

INDIA

Busy Calcutta.
The British-designed yellow Ambassador taxi is the city's emblem.

I've heard that Rickshaws are about to be banned by the Indian Government, as they are considered inhumane. But luckily we still have them in London.

Cows are sacred to India's Hindus and are given extra special treatment as they wander Calcutta.

A British colonial building that now houses a large tree.

Howrah Bridge, which opened in 1943. You are still not allowed to take photos on the bridge without the threat of being arrested.

A spectacular temple and ghat on the banks of the Hooghly River.

Which one is me?

I loved this train, and the view – and the fact that it is an impossible feat of engineering.

The Darjeeling Himalayan Railway heads straight past someone's front door.

Tibetan prayer flags
flutter above the clouds
high in the Himalayas.

Ghoom – the village
with the highest
railway station in
the world.

Hooray! This is what tea pickers look like on the tea packet! Life imitates art!

Rajah and Srirupa's organic tea plantation – I'm drinking the most expensive tea in the world out of antique Japanese cups – so not very relaxing.

Grumpy old Queen Victoria scowls out over Calcutta.

met by Dr Pemba, who remembered happy days at Victoria School in nearby Kurseong. It had been opened by the British in 1879 for the children of lower-ranking government service workers. 'I came there from Tibet in 1941, when I was ten years old, and stayed till I was eighteen. I wanted to go to an English school but the first year was rather unpleasant. My parents said, "You'll be like a fool for a couple of months because you don't speak any English, and if you get teased or get homesick, don't worry. It will be good for you." When we arrived, we went in through the gate and could see boys catching butterflies, playing marbles and hopscotch – all those typical British games. I had to change out of my traditional Tibetan clothes into the school uniform. My first impression was that they were all fair-haired boys and, out of about two hundred boarders, there were only nine or ten of us who were non-British.'

As one of the minority, Dr Pemba was teased for the way he ate and spoke, and he had to adapt to the strange customs of a British public school, such as grace before meals, fagging and cricket. Despite that, he came third in the class at the end of his first year. He was 'speaking very good English and singing songs like "Heart of Oak" and "God Save the King" ', and had begun to enjoy it. As far as he is concerned, his arrival at Victoria School was one of the two turning-points in his life. The other was going to London at eighteen to study medicine at University College. 'I could have gone anywhere but I experienced the whole world of London, the whole English world. So I have no regrets.' Without the British presence in India, his life would have been very different.

From the club, we drove bumpily down the hill, rounding hairpin bends made doubly exciting by the mist that rolled in and out, until we came to the Makaibari Tea Estate, run by Rajah Banarjee, a fifth-generation tea-planter and great-grandson of the original owner. It is the last wholly family-owned tea plantation in the Darjeeling region. Slim, upright, and wearing what looked like army uniform – leather boots, khaki trousers and jacket with deep breast pockets – Rajah took us on a brisk walk though the plantation. A light mist had swept in but the hillside was alive with chirruping crickets. We watched women moving among the bushes, picking the buds and the two leaves that surround them, then tossing them into the sacks they carry on their backs supported by a strap round the forehead.

'As tea drinking became popular in Victorian England, the Chinese decided to put up their prices but the East India Company traders weren't having any of it,' Rajah told us. 'The governor of Hong Kong was inveigled into smuggling out of China tea seeds – *Camellia sinensis* – to be planted in the colonies. Luckily for us, in Darjeeling tea growing boomed and Darjeeling became legendary because anything that grows here has a spectacular flavour. What Darjeeling is to tea, champagne is to wine.'

To begin with, tea-growing was a private enterprise: 'Most of the plantations were British-owned and the investment was all from London. They grew very rapidly, but most of the managers were Scottish. That's why you see some wonderful names like Glenburn, Maggie's Hope and Bannockburn. Those men were quite incredible. There were no roads or communication at all but they somehow got these huge machines – the dryers, the stokers, the withering racks, as well as engines that must have weighed three or four tons – up here. I don't think anyone could do that now. The opening of the railways was another big feat and another private enterprise, run by Gillanders Arbuthnot & Co.'

In the late nineteenth century, there were too few local people to pick the tea, so Nepalese labourers were brought in. They were acclimatised to the mountain atmosphere and hadn't far to come. The contractors hid a few silver coins in the soil between the tea plants to find while they were weeding, so that word would travel and more would join them. 'Everyone says that it was very exploitative,' Rajah said, 'but the farmlands were organised to provide medicine, regular wages, rations and so on. That was not to be found anywhere else in the world and people conveniently forget about that.' He paused. 'The plantations remained largely under British control until Indian independence in 1947, and by the mid-1960s almost all the British planters had left.'

The Banarjees were among the few Indian planters, and Rajah joined his family business in 1970. 'Because the estate was a hundred and sixty years old, we had an immense diversity of plants. I asked, "What is Darjeeling flavour all about?" So for the next two years we did an individual manufacture for more than three thousand plants: we have a small roller in the factory that does that. Each and every tea plant had a different flavour so it dawned on me that the mixing of these various flavours gave the magic and mystique of Darjeeling tea.' Each of the sixty-nine tea estates in Darjeeling produces its own distinctive flavour in the same way that different distilleries produce distinctive single-malt whiskies depending on altitude, the location and genus of the plants.

We were invited into the estate's huge grey factory to watch the production process. The Lord Ganesh, the elephant god, presides over Rajah's estate, so we were all given a scarf bearing his symbol to wear. As we stepped inside, the subtle yet intense aroma of warm Darjeeling tea leaves enveloped us. Rajah explained the simple, yet critical procedures for rolling and drying, then introduced us to his wife, Serupa, who made a pot of 'the world's best tea', Darjeeling Silver Tips. It sells at a world-record $400 per kilo. 'It's a very delicate tea,' Rajah explained, 'and has four layers of flavour that unfold as you roll it along and sip it gently. I normally drink it last thing at night to lull me into celestial slumber.' The delicate blue Japanese cups we used had been presented to Rajah's grandfather in 1872 by aspiring Japanese tea-planters who had come to his estate to learn the trade.

Over more tea in the Banarjees' back garden, surrounded by tall trees and rosebushes, Rajah and Serupa told us about Darjeeling when it had been a British retreat from the heat in Calcutta. Serupa was nostalgic for the 'impeccable standards they set for their homes and for the tea estates. They kept beautiful houses, flower gardens, vegetable gardens, and they had a fabulous social life, regardless of what people might think now. They used to go for walks in the morning, take their dogs out, have a rest in the afternoon. In the evenings they would gather at the club for their card sessions, parties and dances. None of that exists any more.'

'Because Calcutta was the economic capital of the

British,' Rajah added, 'the most powerful aristocrats and bureaucrats had their summer houses up here.'

'The young assistants and some Indians too were at the beck and call of the English ladies,' Serupa went on. But when the women returned to Calcutta, the men were left to their own devices. The resulting illegitimate children were a problem. 'Those children weren't brought up within Indian families but were neglected so Dr Graham Holmes formed an orphanage up here and gave them an education before placing them in different government departments. He did a great social service.'

Today, although the white plantation owners gone, a few British companies dealing in tea are still based in Calcutta. The plantations are now owned either by Indian companies or individuals. But Rajah believed he had benefited from the British presence in India: 'I wouldn't be here if the British hadn't been.' He laughed. 'And neither would the tea.'

~ A Female Sovereign ~

Once her government had accepted responsibility for ruling India, Queen Victoria took charge, showing a depth of imagination that the politicians so clearly lacked. She bullied her ministers into issuing a proclamation to India in 1858, after the Mutiny had ended, from 'a female Sovereign' speaking to them 'on assuming direct rule over them after a bloody civil war' and 'giving them pledges, which her future reign would redeem'. Indian princes were confirmed in their states; there were to be no more conquests or dispossessions. Most importantly, no legal distinctions were to be made between races or religions, and public offices should be open to all. The Queen insisted that all of her subjects were equal.

In 1876 she accepted Prime Minister Benjamin Disraeli's idea that she should be styled Empress of India. In 1877, outside Delhi, Lord Lytton assembled a *durbar*: it was a symbolic enthronement of Victoria as Kaisar-i-Hind, the successor to the Mughal emperor, and all prominent Indian princes attended. Her Indian subjects revered the Great White Queen perhaps because she was eight thousand miles away: they might have felt differently if they had had to deal in person with her as she grew into tetchy old age. Remote from the disturbing reality, Victoria loved the idea of India, as represented by her attendant, Abdul Karim, the 'Munshi'. She rebuked Lord Salisbury for referring to Indians as 'black men' and for his 'harsh, crushing policy'. In this she reflected the opinions of the British public, but not necessarily those of the British in India.

Queen Victoria attended by the Munshi

∿ *Anglo-Saxon Habits* ∿

Under the British Raj, Indians were able, for the first time in their history, to communicate in the same language, which they have since adopted and made their own. With the language, however, came British ideas, not all of which were welcome. Equality before the law (there was no any acceptance of social equality because the Victorian British were incurably snobbish) offended Brahmins, who found themselves on the same legal rung of the ladder as Untouchables, and Muslims, whose word was suddenly judged to be worth no more than that of a Hindu.

One powerful influence for national unity and social equality came from the gradual involvement of Indians in the quintessentially English game of cricket. In 1850 The Parsi community, always readier to adapt to new customs than Indians of other faiths, had founded the Young Zoroastrian Club in Bombay. In 1886 its cricket team toured England, winning eight and losing eleven matches, a respectable set of results. Three years later an English touring side, which included the famous batsman Lord Hawke, captain of Yorkshire, visited India: after a triumphant tour, which included thrashing the white Bombay Gymkhana side, the visitors were soundly defeated by the Zoroastrians, and the young Parsis celebrated victory 'over the victors of Waterloo'. In 1952 India won its first ever Test match – against England.

∿ *The End of Empire* ∿

The history of India from the Mughal Empire, through the British Raj, to Indian independence on 15 August 1947, is illustrated by the Nehru family. The father of Motilal Nehru, a successful barrister (1861–1931), was a Mughal official; Motilal's son Jawaharlal (1889–1964, Harrow, Cambridge and the Inner Temple) became the first prime minister of the Indian Republic, which he had done so much to establish; his sister, Vijaya Pandit, represented India, still a Commonwealth member, as high commissioner in London; his daughter Indira Gandhi succeeded him as prime minister in 1966, and her son, Rajiv, followed in 1984. Motilal and his son died peacefully in their beds, but Indira and Rajiv Gandhi were assassinated by local extremists: a cruel example of the tensions that broke out following the retreat of the British Raj.

India had secured independence with her contribution in the Second World War, but it was achieved at the price of violent division between Hindu India and Muslim Pakistan. The new India incorporated British customs, such as social democracy, cricket (Nehru was an amateur player), a free press, the rule of law and the English language, within the complex of venerable Indian traditions and ideas. On the other hand, curry has become the British national food, and Indians own some 10 per cent of British assets. Perhaps that is a mutually satisfactory result after three centuries of co-existence.

We left the relative cool of the mighty Himalayan foothills to return south to Calcutta. We had been given snapshots of India during the days of the East India Company and under British rule, and now we wanted to discover what the British legacy to India had been. This time we found

Toby Sinclair in the Coffee House. Over the years, eminent writers, revolutionaries and poets, among them Rabindranath Tagore, have come here to observe the time-honoured Bengali tradition of *adda*, or intellectual exchange. The walls are plastered with posters advertising Calcutta's cultural events – and never entirely removed. The shreds are merely covered with new ones. The Coffee House reminded us of a set in a Ridley Scott film: what you can see of the walls has faded to various shades of brown, and ancient black metal ceiling fans whir over dark wooden tables and chairs. The waiters hover in flawless white uniforms. The modest menu is displayed on a board above the till and the graffiti is in English.

The Coffee House was buzzing as we asked Toby if the British had been arrogant in their attitude to India and in the way they had imposed their values. 'Arrogant is the right word,' he agreed. 'It applies to many parts of the world where they imposed their society. But there are many people in Calcutta who see the British way of life as the high point of culture and superior to theirs. That makes me sad because Indian history and culture are so marvellous. However, there are many positive legacies, the greatest of which is the English language, which gives India a building block for the future in the twenty-first century. A large percentage of the population is still educated in English and all university education is conducted in English. India can go out into the world of information technology, medical technology and so forth at the same time as all the back-room work required by the world – for example, call centres – is becoming centred here. It is cheaper for a multinational company to use the educated English-speaking work-force they find here.'

But wasn't the British Empire founded on cheap labour? 'It's cheaper labour here than in Britain, but the people working in Mumbai, Bangalore or Calcutta are earning considerably more than they likely would in a local bank or office. So it benefits both parties. The country is producing more graduates in the English language than any other outside the United States so there's a huge pop-ulation looking for jobs. The West needs their skills and it's cheaper to have them doing the work here at the end of a telephone line than it is to bring an immigrant work-force into Britain.

'What other nation with a population of a billion can look so positively into the future?' he reflected. 'India is a proud nation, and a great nation that has matched its cul-ture with empire and created a modern country. The legal structure and the railway infrastructure are other positive British legacies. There are, of course, some negative aspects too – some draconian laws haven't been taken off the statute book: land-reform ownership laws, tax laws and police-control laws in some parts of the country.' Incidentally, as a film crew we had been brought face to face with just such a draconian law when we discovered a piece of legislation established during the Second World War that meant we couldn't film anything from or towards a bridge, on pain of spending the night in a police cell.

During the years Toby has lived in India, he has enjoyed the tolerance that was extended to the traders three centuries ago. 'I try hard not to take advantage of that,' he admitted. 'I'm part of the Indian system and the laws apply to me as much as to anyone else in this coffee shop.'

In contrast to the sea of people living and working on the streets, large colonial buildings offer a vision of the city's former grandeur. Calcutta was once known as 'City of Palaces'. Among the narrow streets, huge derelict buildings overshadow simpler dwellings, the crumbling grandeur squeezed beside everyday life. Their cracked Palladian pillars, rusting wrought-iron balconies, overgrown courtyards and plump white statues now green with lichen, are still telling reminders of Calcutta's glorious past. The Victoria Memorial is one of the most celebrated – a white marble palace, now an art gallery, with domes, towers and gardens. Although it is one of the most impressive buildings in Calcutta, its formality robs it of atmosphere – plump Queen Victoria is seated squarely on her throne overlooking the formal gardens, where families and lovers wander in the cool of evening. When we were there, shortly after a bomb had exploded just outside the city, the government had closed all national monuments to the public so we were restricted to filming the palace from the street, but its size and grandeur left us in no doubt that the British had intended those who saw it to grasp that they were not merely an occupying force: they felt they 'owned' India and that they were here to stay.

5

Hong Kong

What you never see on these documentaries, and it would get very tedious if you did, is the huge amount of faffing that goes on with the bags. We had forty-five bits of luggage, which all had to be checked in, X-rayed, and pushed from terminal to terminal in great tottering heaps. Some were massive great bits that were forever falling off the trolley or sweeping some tiny old tourist off her spindly ankles; others were misleadingly small ludicrously heavy flight bags about the size of a vanity case and weighing a bit more than a Ford Fiesta.

We seemed to do most of our checking in at three thirty in the morning, and we seemed to arrive everywhere in the middle of the night. There would always be a big flurry of excited bustle as the first forty-three pieces of gear came round on the carousel – we'd be lined up with our trolleys like mothers in the egg-and-spoon race, and bags and boxes would be stacked up, counted off, counted off again by someone else; lists would be consulted, and then it would dawn slowly on all of us that something vital, like a box of lenses, or yesterday's rushes, had not come through and that we were in for a long wait.

The girls on the team would usually slump in a corner, conserving energy, but the men would carry on striding about, counting, checking and often stacking up the bags in a different formation, as if that would make them add up to the right number. More often than not, after a fraught forty-five minutes, someone would remember that the blue bag was inside the

126

black box, or that the lenses had gone in with the sandwiches, and that we did, in fact, have everything. The trolleys would then be lined up for the last time, we'd have one final round of striding, counting and, as a stylish finishing touch, some sharp slapping of each pile, a sort of on-you-go type smack, as if the trolleys were about to go into the show ring, and only then would we be ready to leave the airport and film another country.

Hong Kong was grey and humid. It was the first hotel on this trip that had a gym, and I felt very cosmopolitan on my cross trainer – if I looked out through the window I could see the harbour surrounded by skyscrapers, and if I looked at the television, I could see Anne Robinson on *The Weakest Link* serving up tortuous one-liners with all the enthusiasm and vitality of someone waiting for another go on the thumbscrews.

I couldn't really get a handle on Hong Kong – it seemed to be all about money and shopping, and the shops were the same as the ones at home. And there didn't seem to be anywhere to go that wasn't shops, not in the time that we had available anyway. We went up to Victoria Peak on the tram, which I enjoyed, I do like a tram ride, but at the top it was just more shops, and a Madame Tussaud's. There was a rubbish Princess Anne and a terrible Princess Di, and a not-bad Benny Hill. And that was it really: money, shops and Fred Scuttle immortalised in wax, saluting.

∽ Introduction ∽

For much of its history, China had traditionally refused to allow any but the most restricted foreign trade. This, together with the illegal smuggling of opium, led to war with Britain in 1841. The island of Hong Kong became a British colony and foreign merchants were admitted to four other Chinese ports. With the immigration of enterprising Chinese, British-run Hong Kong became prosperous,

The Union Flag raised on Hong Kong

gradually expanding on to the 'New Territories' of the main-land. After the Second World War and the Communist takeover of China, millions of refugees fled to Hong Kong, furthering its astonishing economic success. As the expiry date of the New Territories' lease approached, negotiations with China resulted in the British handover of the colony, which is today acknowledged as one of the world's major business centres.

Hong Kong is a twenty-four-hour city and we had only forty-eight hours in which to get used to it. We were plunged straight into a chaos of people eating as they talked on mobile phones, rushing to their next appoint-ment, making money without a moment to spare. Calcutta had been crowded and noisy but it was spiritual and friendly too. The overwhelming impression we gained of Hong Kong was of energy, power, money and trade.

The roar of traffic and the hum of electricity are aug-mented during the day by jack-hammers working on new skyscrapers. Money is king: everywhere, vast neon hoard-ings wink down, encouraging people to spend. They make Piccadilly Circus look like Toy Town. Thousands of taxis hare about like giant red beetles, taking yet more people to yet more places where they can spend yet more money. Hong Kong seemed a hard city with sharp edges: the buildings were impossibly tall and too tightly packed, and the whole place was lit up like a beacon.

We began our first evening with a water tour of Victoria Harbour where every night at eight o'clock the twenty-minute 'Symphony of Lights' takes place under the inky-blue sky with coloured lasers shooting from the rooftops of thirty-three buildings on the Hong Kong and Kowloon waterfronts. On the boat, we met Peter Moss, a resident of Hong Kong since 1965. He had recently retired after working for twenty-eight years with the Hong Kong government, and is presently director of editorial services at Salon Films, and author of a number of books, including *Passing Shadows Hong Kong*. As we rocked on the choppy harbour waters, he started to tell us how the opium trade had led China to cede Hong Kong to Britain.

'It was a story of British greed and Chinese obstinacy that started with the British addiction to tea and the Chinese addiction to opium. When the British discovered how much the Chinese needed opium, they grew it in India, specifically to overcome the Chinese embargo on trade with Britain. When the Chinese banned opium the British traded it under the counter for tea and other goods. Eventually the Chinese emperor put a stop to this by burning the opium stocks that had accumulated in British warehouses. This led to the first Opium War. The British won and, in 1842, Hong Kong was ceded to Britain in perpetuity. But that was not the end of the matter. In 1856 the second Opium War broke out after the "Arrow Incident" in which Chinese officials boarded the Arrow, a ship recently registered as British, arrested members of the crew and hauled down the British ensign. The British governor was so furious, he demanded we go to war again, creating the pretext for giving Kowloon, in the New Territories, to Britain.'

At last Britain had a toehold on the Chinese mainland, which was important because they couldn't grow sufficient crops on the island to sustain Hong Kong, but they were still worried that other imperial powers might step in. 'That led to the 1898 lease of the New Territories for ninety-nine years. Although we started out with the intention of using them as a sterile zone, we inevitably spilled over into them increasingly so they became effectively amalgamated with Kowloon and Hong Kong. When China wanted to end the lease, the airport was in the New Territories as well as nearly all the factories and two-thirds of the population. We couldn't sever the New Territories from Hong Kong so we had to give the whole lot back.'

∼ An Opium War? ∼

In September 1660 Samuel Pepys was one of the first to try 'a cup of tee, a China drink', which 'I had never drunk before'. At first it was just a fashionable drink, but by the early years of the nineteenth century it had become a national habit, even supplanting beer at breakfast. Duty on tea, then available only from China, brought the British government some £3 million a year, which represented nearly a tenth of its annual income.

Trading with China had been difficult for foreigners since the end of the fifteenth century when the Ming emperors had pulled down the shutters on all seaborne commerce. Three hundred years later only the port of Canton, at the head of the Pearl river estuary, was open to foreign traders, and then – in theory at least – under strict control. A further complication was that the Chinese had developed an addiction to opium that was even stronger than that of the British to tea, and opium was produced profitably by the British East India Company in Bengal. But while tea imports produced a substantial income for the British government, the Chinese authorities earned nothing from the opium trade, which had been officially illegal since 1729. The ban did not prevent Canton merchants from accepting as much as foreign traders, mainly British and American, could supply. Canton was a long way from the capital, Peking, and imperial edicts were ignored.

Under the supervision of a committee of British merchants appointed by the East India Company, the trade in Canton was carried on, usually in a dignified manner. In 1833, however, the Company's charter was altered to terminate all its trading activities, thereby creating a free-for-all on the Pearl river. The British government decided to appoint an official 'invested by law with adequate powers of supervision over all British subjects'. The Chinese government was not consulted. The first such 'Superintendent of Trade', Lord Napier, infuriated the Chinese with his high-handed attitude and was humiliatingly expelled. He was replaced in 1836 by his junior, Captain Charles Elliot – a cousin of Governor General Lord Auckland – who was soon faced with a crisis.

In December 1838, after a long debate on legitimising the trade, the Tao-kuang (Daoguang) emperor decided to appoint the incorruptible and brave mandarin Lin Tse-hsü to abolish it. Lin descended on Canton, threatening Chinese and foreign merchants alike, collected all of the available opium, more than a thousand tonnes, and burned it. He also made the great mistake of attempting to arrest the man he considered the most important trader, Lancelot Dent.

To the Foreign Secretary Lord Palmerston, this insult to a

British subject was an intolerable affront. He accepted the Chinese right to confiscate the opium but could not tolerate Lin's strong-arm methods and demanded compensation. After all, opium was legal in Britain. During the subsequent months of negotiation the British community was forced out of Canton and Macao to find what shelter it could among the ships moored in the safe haven of Hong Kong. When at last an expeditionary force arrived from England, Captain Elliot, anxious not to protract hostilities, 'with its certain consequence of deep hatred', offered the Chinese a demonstration of British power. In a single day, with the help of the East India Company's armed steamer *Nemesis*, he destroyed the supposedly impregnable river defences of Canton, and the city lay open to a British assault. Within a week negotiations were in full swing, and a fortnight later the Chinese envoys had agreed to Elliot's demands: $6 million plus the 'barren island' of Hong Kong to compensate for the loss of the opium.

∼ *Queen Victoria is Amused* ∼

In April 1841 when she heard that Hong Kong had been added to her already extensive empire, the Queen agreed with Prince Albert that their baby daughter should be styled 'Princess of Hong Kong' in addition to 'Princess Royal' – this being her idea of a joke. However, the Foreign Secretary, Lord Palmerston, was 'greatly mortified and disappointed' that Captain Elliot had won only 'a barren island with hardly a house on it. It seems obvious that Hong Kong will never be a Mart of Trade . . .' Elliot was recalled, and given the least attractive job in the British diplomatic service: ambassador to the Republic of Texas.

If Palmerston was wrong in his assessment of Hong Kong's future, his description was confirmed by the Chinese officials who informed the Emperor that Hong Kong was indeed a 'barren island comprising many rocky peaks . . . isolated in the sea some one hundred li from the chief town of Xia'n County . . . formerly a lair for pirates and almost uninhabited'. The Emperor raised no objection to the British remaining on the island provided that – he insisted – the Chinese authorities could collect customs duties. It was a vain hope and the subject was allowed to die.

The town of Victoria: one of the world's finest harbours

As a professional naval officer Elliot had immediately appreciated that Hong Kong's harbour was one of the world's finest, easily defensible, and that it would make a much better centre for trade than Canton. The Union flag was hoisted on the shore of what would become the city of Victoria on 26 January 1841. When it was hauled down in 1997, Hong Kong had become one of the richest cities in the world.

∼ *This Singular People* ∼

Inevitably, the French looked for ways to intrude. Mallet de Basillan, a secret agent sent to Canton in 1839, was soon spotted and teased mercilessly by the younger merchants; he never saw the joke and reported that a plot was afoot to destroy the Chinese Emperor and to place a young British trader Robert Thom, on the throne. More conventionally, in 1843 the captain of a French warship offered to help China in her struggle against the British imperialists by teaching her people to build ships and cannons and to fight at sea. He was politely rejected; the Chinese knew what had happened at the battle of Trafalgar.

The first Opium War was officially concluded in August 1842, without the import of opium becoming legal, but with smuggling now much more widespread since Sir Henry Pottinger, Captain Elliot's successor, had secured another valuable advantage. He had gained permission for all foreign merchants to trade in four more Chinese ports including Shanghai, the 'Treaty Ports', where Chinese were allowed to mingle with 'foreign barbarians'. With this concession, the British government wondered whether it needed to hold on to Hong Kong. Lord Aberdeen, the then foreign secretary, a cautious soul, saw only the disadvantages: retention of Hong Kong would 'be attended with great and certain expense'.

He also worried that possession of the island might '. . . also tend to bring us more in contact politically with the Chinese than is at all desirable; and might ultimately lead, perhaps unavoidably, to our taking part in the contest and changes which at no distant period may occur among this singular people, and in the government of the Empire.'

~ A Good Bargain ~

In 1856, with the Taiping rebellion that devastated much of southern China, Lord Aberdeen's worries were justified. The Hong Kong governor, Dr John Bowring, and Harry Parkes, the British consul at Canton, provoked a war that was only terminated in 1860. Bowring had been editor of the influential *Westminster Review*, but he was also pompous and conceited, with no experience of service abroad. However, he had served as a Whig MP, meaning that a job had to be found for him, in spite of his unpopularity – Palmerston called him 'Quack Dr Bowring'. The twenty-eight-year-old Parkes was equally sure of himself and more than ready to ignore any official limits on his authority. As Governor and Consul, the two men used a diplomatic incident to force a quarrel with the Chinese governor of Canton.

The conflict they ignited was known variously as the Arrow War (since it began with the Chinese seizure of a British-registered ship) or, misleadingly, the Second Opium War. It was settled only after full-scale combat and the occupation of Peking by a force under British plenipotentiary Lord Elgin. The reclusive Chinese Emperor was forced to allow free travel and trade throughout his realm to all foreigners, who were to remain subject only to their own nations' laws. In retaliation for the murder of some Europeans, including the *Times*'s correspondent Thomas Bowlby, who had been starved, then beaten to death, Elgin ordered the Imperial Summer Palace to be destroyed, an act of vandalism that fuelled lasting Chinese resentment.

The New Elgin Marbles: Lord Elgin plays with cannon balls against the Chinese

Almost as an aside, the mainland shore opposite Victoria, part of the Chinese town of Kowloon, was transferred to British sovereignty for $500 in a personal deal between Parkes and the Chinese Governor General of Canton. For that modest sum the colony gained security – a battery mounted there could close the harbour – and the valuable piece of real estate known as Tsimshatsui.

Hong Kong has developed from a virtually barren rock inhabited by four thousand fishermen to the enormously successful, crowded financial epicentre that it is today. Curious to find out what life had been like for the British when they first arrived, we talked to Dan Waters, who has lived in Hong Kong since 1954, and retired from its education department in 1980. We met him on Victoria Peak, having taken the seven-minute tram ride to the summit where we could look out over the Hong Kong and Kowloon skylines.

Dan has written widely on local history, culture and customs, and has served on the Government Antiquities Advisory Board. He is also president of the Royal Asiatic Society, Hong Kong Branch. In the sticky heat of early morning, he contemplated Hong Kong's extraordinary growth: 'To a large extent it was the drive of the Chinese but, of course, the British system of law and order was laid over the top.' Trade had been attracted to the island because business was done under British contracts, which could be trusted. 'When I came here, the population was two-and-a-half million, ten years later it was three-and-a-half million and today there's around seven million. The Chinese came here because they thought they could earn a better living than on the mainland. This is changing now that there are far better opportunities on the mainland than there used to be and, of course, our lawyers are now going over to work in China. Things are improving there.'

When the British arrived on the island, 'There were two main fishing villages – Stanley and Aberdeen. It was a rural place with a bit of agriculture but largely fishing. The British came ashore on 25 January 1841. They reboarded their ship that night but returned the following day for a special ceremony at Procession Point where they hoisted the flag and gave three cheers for Her Majesty Queen Victoria. There were no houses to speak of so the early British built mat sheds based on a skeleton of bamboo. Unfortunately they were all blown down in a bad typhoon. For water, they had Waterfall Bay but, to a large extent, they dug wells and depended on streams. They bought their food from local villagers. The early settlers were merchants from Macau and Canton. Firms such as Jardine Matheson, Gibb Livingstone and Watson's were all established in Canton before they came to Hong Kong.'

Dan was in no doubt that life for those early incomers had been tough. 'The British were hit by ill-health, succumbing to plague, cholera and other tropical diseases. Many are buried in the old Colonial Cemetery, renamed the Hong Kong Cemetery in 1972.' However, those who survived achieved a huge amount very quickly. 'In the old days they used to say that when the British went somewhere to set up a colony, they did three things. They built a church – here we have St John's Cathedral on Garden Road. They set up a racecourse – here it's at Happy Valley. They planted botanical gardens. They did all this within their first decade in Hong Kong. The army – the engineers – played a big part in designing the buildings. Some of the old army buildings, such as Murray House and Flagstaff House, were built in the first decade. They settled down quickly.' Although the Chinese and Europeans were often socially segregated, they mixed for business. Because most Europeans couldn't speak Cantonese, they had compradore, local agents who were at home in both languages and could facilitate transactions. 'Typical was Sir Robert Hotung who died aged ninety-three in 1956. He was the first non-European to live on the Peak, which until then had been exclusively for British people.

'The Chinese left their wives at home, as did the European until about the 1870s when the Peak became a residential area for the British. There were many strictly segregated licensed brothels, which were phased out for the Europeans in 1932 and for the Chinese in 1936. Of course, there were illegal brothels too. There was a garrison here right from the start, and later on a police force was established. It kept order although a lot of corruption went on. There were no lawyers at all to begin with. People believed that if you wanted something, you had to pay for it. A bribe could get you out of anything. I remember a woman telling me that two policemen had caught her grandfather smoking opium. He gave them each twenty dollars, which was quite a lot in those days, and it was all forgotten.

'Corruption was endemic in Chinese society and people latched on to the local way of life. It continued until 1974 when Peter Godber, a police officer, was discovered to have been taking massive sums of money. That's when Lord Maclehose set up the Independent Commission Against Corruption.'

We asked Dan whether our impression that Hong Kong society is ruled by money, was correct. 'To a large extent, yes,' he replied. 'But not entirely, because people here are very generous. They believe that if you're generous on earth, you'll be looked after when you die.' To us, that sounded oddly like a bribe to heaven.

∾ Business and Pleasure ∾

Although foreign trade was now largely permitted, Hong Kong remained the only city in China under foreign sovereignty where transactions could be carried out under English law, staffed by effective and, at higher levels, honest officials, in much greater safety than anywhere else in China. The Hongkong and Shanghai Banking Corporation (HSBC), one of the world's biggest banks, was founded there in 1865 by Thomas Sutherland, recommended by his previous employer as 'a thorough man of business and not too Scotch'.

Britannia offers an alarmed Emperor gunpowder tea while France looks on

Hong Kong attracted Europeans and Chinese alike, but forty years after the colony's foundation, ninety-five per cent of the population was Chinese. Victoria was essentially a Chinese city under British administration, which created problems for those who looked for democracy, a concept then unknown in China. The best that Colonial Secretary Henry Labouchere could offer was that 'respectable Chinese' would be appointed to the administration alongside British officials, and eventually, in the 1880s, two Chinese barristers were appointed to the Legislative Council. However, the races led separate lives, meeting socially only on formal occasions. Representation of all sections of the 'respectable' community, appointed by the Governor but not by election, was to continue as Hong Kong's principle of government.

It was generally assured at this time that 'subject peoples' would be so impressed by the superior British administration that they would copy British habits, diet and tailoring. To some extent this was so: once independent, former colonies retained British law and the English language, and many continued to play cricket. But the Chinese, conscious of their ancient civilisation, remained unimpressed. They had, it was claimed, 'the best drink in the world, tea; the best food in the world, rice; and the best clothing in the world, silk'. What did they need from the West?

Although the Chinese valued the security and freedom that came with the British administration, many insisted on retaining their own traditions. Since these included child-marriage, an almost complete lack of public hygiene, such institutions as the I Ts'z, a place set aside for people to die in without inconveniencing their relatives, and such customs as mui-tsai, female indentured servitude that sounded suspiciously like slavery, the colonial authorities had to tread warily. Venereal disease was endemic, but the existence of brothels could not be admitted to the British public. There was no argument, however, against banning them and the Hong Kong magistrates agreed to close down those that did not permit their girls to be medically examined. The existence of the others was not mentioned. Hong Kong was never going to fulfil Victorian ideals.

In November 1869 the colony received its first royal visitor in Queen Victoria's second son, Prince Alfred, Duke of Edinburgh. He was entertained by the Amateur Dramatic Corps, and the German choir at the new City Hall Theatre.

The races at Happy Valley: 'all the amenities of home'

As he was a competent violinist, he conducted another concert himself, and also attended a Chinese theatre, played cricket and bowls, and laid the foundation of the new Anglican cathedral's chancel.

Less respectable visitors could enjoy 'excellent sherry cob-blers', a newly invented 'cocktail' at an American bar, while the serious-minded appreciated the library and reading rooms, where they might play chess, practise music or attend lectures. With the racetrack at Happy Valley, Hong Kong had all the amenities of home.

∾ *Treaty Ports* ∾

The British colony and the Treaty Ports now open to foreign trade offered two further advantages to the Chinese populace – the first being the freedom to leave China. A flood of Chinese took ship in the beginning of the Chinese diaspora that has done so much to improve the West's prosperity – and its cuisine. Conditions among some of the ships on the 'Pig Trade' were deplorable: on one voyage, 128 of the 332 embarked committed suicide, but Bowring, the governor of Hong Kong, insisted that certain minimum standards should be observed, including the provision of a surgeon. Most of the Chinese emigrants chose British colonies or America as their destination, and it was not long before the West Indies, South Africa and Australia had a Chinese community.

Hong Kong institutions allowed a small number of Chinese to enter English-speaking political society, then take their place on the world stage. Dr Sun Yat Sen, the founder of the Chinese Republic, was an early graduate of Dr Mawson's College of Medicine in Hong Kong. In 1895, Sun, with the support of Sir Ch'i Ho Ch'i, and the discreet approval of the governor, Sir Henry Black, made Hong Kong the centre of revolutionary conspiracies against the Ch'ing regime that prevailed in China.

Taking advantage of China's defeat by modern Japanese forces in 1895, the Western powers demanded concessions from the shaken Chinese.

Russia obtained a new harbour at Port Arthur; the German representative at Peking, whom the Kaiser had told to act, if need be, 'with the most brutal ruthlessness', succeeded in extorting a substantial slice of Chinese territory around Tsingtao, where the flourishing Chinese brewing industry was begun; France had already selected Kwang-chou Bay as a naval station. These developments alarmed the British government, which, while supporting the integrity of China, suggested that 'a slight extension to the territory of Hong Kong' would not go amiss.

Back on the waterfront, we had arranged to meet Lamy Li, a native Hongkongese, to find out what what makes the city tick. 'We are very hard-working, very materialistic and very optimistic, always looking forward. We are not as sentimental about the past as the West, and are proud of the new. New is modern and better. We are proud to show off our wealth. In Chinese we have a saying: "If you are wealthy but not showing off your wealth, it's like wearing a nice dress and walking in the dark." Why not show it off? Then your friends and family can be proud of you. In Hong Kong we say, "We don't have dreams, we have plans." Having money is the essential element of happiness in this city.'

We had been surprised not to see any children in the city. 'Most of us have none or only one child,' said Lamy. 'If you have only one, you try to protect them as much as possible. We work so hard to try to send them into a very nice school, get them the best you can wear and so on. It's a competition between the children – how they dress, what they have, where they go on vacation, et cetera. In some ways people are more interested in their lifestyle. It's not as bad as it sounds. I think it's the best motivation to keep you ahead.'

Lamy was brought up on the island. Her father was a policeman and three of her uncles were in the British Army. As a result she was always aware of the differences between a Chinese local, a Hongkongese and a Westerner, and saw what the different members of her family experienced as typical. 'You can put in the same effort or offer the same service but you wouldn't get the same sort of treatment and respect. Because we did not have a real nationality. We weren't British in a British colony and, in a way, we were not Chinese. We had an identity crisis. Money is our only way of grabbing a sense of security.' Everything is based on how much a person has: if you have money, you can rise to the top. 'A lot of rich, highly respected people haven't had any proper education,' she told us. Because the whole city is based on business success, and it is a stressful place to live. Many of Lamy's friends have more than one job and put in at least a six-day week with everyone working overtime to pay their mortgage. She explained that people expect to do better than their parents. 'It's a good motivation again. Instead of just keeping your child happy, we have to make sure our parents live well after they've retired. Family is our first responsibility.'

There doesn't seem to be much time for a social life – one day a week, if you're lucky – so it can be hard to start a relationship or find a husband or wife. 'Everyone is so busy, so you either find someone in your office, within your neighbourhood or you have to wait for a chance. Hong Kong girls concentrate too much on their work to prove they are strong enough to compete with men. Men don't like that and lately a lot of men travel to China, some to work and some to have fun, and they meet someone they like on the mainland where the girls are more gentle, more traditional and more willing to stay at home.' But even if you have a husband, life can be difficult. 'A lot of married men go and look for someone who can offer them comfort. It has turned into a major social issue since China opened up their gate to Hong Kong people.'

As for the British legacy to Hong Kong, Lamy felt its most positive aspect was the legal system: 'This place is very safe and the law is pretty fair, allowing us to enjoy a certain level of freedom.' But, she added, there was a negative side: 'It's the feeling of being a second-class citizen in your own town. But since 1997 it has been a lot better. I feel that now I can stand up and say I am Chinese Hong Kong.'

∼ 1997 ∼

The 'slight extension' requested by the British government in 1898 was an area of a thousand square kilometres, just a little smaller than Bedfordshire. The extent of the 'New Territories' was primarily determined by tactical considerations, most important being the need to protect the harbour, since artillery had by then a twenty-mile range. Unlike Hong Kong Island, ceded in perpetuity, or Harry Parkes's bargain over Kowloon, the New Territories were leased from China for a period of ninety-nine years, to run from August 1898.

At that time no one could have foreseen Hong Kong's explosive expansion after the Second World War. The Hong Kong government managed, with immense effort, to accommodate all the newcomers, mainly in the New Territories, which became an integral part of the colony. The enterprise of the new arrivals guaranteed its phenomenal economic success.

As termination of the lease approached, discussions took place with China on the colony's future, and continued for twenty years, sometimes acrimoniously and nearly failing altogether after the 1989 massacre in Tiananmen Square. It was eventually agreed that the entire colony would be handed back to China when the lease expired. On 1 July 1997, in drenching rain, the governor, Christopher Patten, saw the Union flag lowered for the last time, and the inauguration of the Special Administrative Region of the People's Republic of China. Hong Kong's prosperity has continued undiminished.

The Prince of Wales and Mr Patten respond to the loyal toast

Lamy took us to see how people spent their money. Our first stop was China Treasure, which was jammed with antiques. Lamy picked up a traditional ceramic pillow, which raised a woman's head to protect her hairdo while she slept. She explained that, surprisingly, the customers were mostly ex-pats and Westerners: 'They're more interested in the local culture and have bigger apartments. You need a big place to put all this and we're pretty practical. For example, we prefer IKEA because it's cheaper and it fits. Every penny we spend, we make sure it's worth it.' She looked at a mah-jong set priced at $2000 (£130) and laughed. 'I would go for a plastic one costing two hundred (£13). It's hard to make money here and in Hong Kong it's all about how you fit in society. We Chinese say: "We'll respect your outfit before we respect you." So to earn someone's respect, you've got to dress well. It doesn't matter how you furnish your home so we keep them simple and seldom invite people to them because they're so small. That's why the restaurants are packed. Check it out!'

Shopping is high on every Hong Kong dweller's agenda, and impressive modern malls cater to every whim. In a bathroom shop we found a solid gold loo complete with gem-studded U-bend – could this be the pinnacle of financial success?

On the way we called at the Tai Cheong Bakery to try their renowned custard tarts sometimes known as 'Fat Pattens', because while Christopher Patten was governor, he was a frequent customer. They were delicious – light pastry with a warm creamy filling.

We went on to the Chinese Veterinary Medicine Hospital. The surgery was clinical, strip-lit, with pets and owners waiting quietly to see Hermie. One patient, a large tortoise, trundled about the waiting room, and stopped to nibble a rucksack.

The clinic walls were covered with newpaper cuttings about Hermie's success with her patients – some had recovered enough to win 'best of show'. That day the first was a very furry cat that needed acupuncture. Hermie took it into her treatment room and laid it on the table. And she stuck needles into it, its eyes closed. 'This treatment is for liver cancer,' Hermie explained. 'We're trying to make the blood circulation better, so he can walk around and play a bit more.'

Veterinary care doesn't come cheap, but Hong Kong people love their pets. They might save for a tailor-made dog's bed costing $3000 (about £195). Hermie agreed with Lamy that they are too busy to have children so lavish affection on animals instead. 'People work long hours, sometimes from nine in the morning until eleven at night. If they have kids, they won't have time to take care of them or even communicate with them. You have to teach them how to study and look at their homework too. But if they have pets they can go home, feed them and go to sleep.'

This seemed to us like a high price to pay, but Hermie told us that recent research had shown that the average cost of bringing up a child until they were eighteen costs HK$4 million. 'When people hear this figure, they freak out. No way!' A small pet is the cheaper alternative. 'Because our houses are small, the popular breeds in Hong Kong are Pomeranian, Chihuahua or Schnauzer.' She was anxious to point out that the Chinese practice of eating dog does not take place in Hong Kong, thanks to the British who brought with them the pet culture. 'If Chinese people are rich they may buy a beautiful dog and a very healthy one and they will cook them. In Hong Kong not many people would do it but some people from China might have this idea.'

Apparently, for the Chinese, a pet is much like a disposable fashion accessory and status symbol. When a new breed of dog is imported and becomes fashionable, 'They will just throw away the old one and buy a new one. They like showing that "I have plenty of money to buy a new breed." They just let them into the street and don't care if they are hit by a car. They don't care how the animal feels. In China, if you want a popular dog, you pay a lot of money for it and for the licence. It means you are very rich.'

We were amazed by the variety of Chinese cultural activities that took place on the island. During China's Cultural Revolution, Hong Kong became a refuge for mainland Chinese, thanks to the relaxed British attitude. We saw t'ai chi being practised by a master on the waterfront, his red silk outfit fluttering in the evening breeze. In Kowloon we watched traditional street opera, an ancient art form that has been kept alive in Hong Kong. The Chinese opera was a rich night-time spectacle: the area was lit by colourful lanterns and torches, while men and women in silk costumes sang and mimed on a raised bamboo stage. Their faces were ghostly white, their eyes, cheeks and lips boldly painted. Below the stage a crowd listened to songs of their heritage.

Finally we visited the Wong Tai Sin Taoist temple, now dwarfed by the surrounding skyscrapers. At the heart of the huge complex people of all ages were praying on a vast forecourt, some on their knees in the hot sun, with a pile of fruit as an offering to a dead ancestor, others buying and lighting incense sticks, then taking them to the main altar. All of this was accompanied by the sound of a gong, and the clatter of fortune sticks. Stalls near the temple offer palm-readings, too – in Hong Kong the future matters, not the past.

6

Borneo

Our sixth and hottest country. We drove to the Gomantong Caves, and walked across a clearing to the cave entrance. It was so hot that even the people who lived there seemed poleaxed. The cave felt like a discount warehouse for germs. The floor was inches deep in bat guano, which is a popular breeding medium for cockroaches. There were all sorts of things scuttling about – my makeup girl primarily, scuttling out into the open air, and who could blame her. We were here to see the collecting of the discarded swiftlet nests. And why would that be? Because they are the nests from which birds' nest soup is made. They are worth an absolute fortune, and you can only collect them if you have a licence from the government. And nerves of steel, because the nests are high up in the roof of the cave and can only be harvested using rope-ladders and bamboo canes. It's a very skilled and dangerous occupation.

Which we didn't film. Because the men who collect the nests weren't there. They were there another day. A day when we were filming a wax effigy of Benny Hill possibly, or slapping luggage in an airport. But I did pick up a piece of nest, and was disappointed that it wasn't the round twiggy thing beloved of the *Beano*.

All this was working up to me having to eat some of the blithering soup. I couldn't quite decide where it fitted in with my vegetarianism. The valuable ingredient is the swiftlet saliva, which sticks the bits of nest together. So, really, it's a bowl of hotted-up bird spit and an Oxo cube. I didn't want to have it at all, but when a whole camera crew has slogged through the heat to film the cave preamble it seemed a bit feeble not to taste it. And it's not as if it was platypus penis or anything. I had a bit. It looked like sperm and the soup tasted of sugar, and I couldn't quite see why you'd want it as the centrepiece of your wedding buffet when Edna Baxter and the like are doing something nutritious in a can for a fraction of the price. But, then, on my wedding day I had spaghetti on toast.

Flying home from Borneo I switched on the in-flight entertainment, and there on the screen was a familiar bat-dropping-encrusted location. High up in the roof, men on rope-ladders were dislodging swiftlet nests to the sonorous accompaniment of a well-loved voice. David flipping Attenborough, he's been everywhere.

∾ *Introduction* ∾

Contemporary Borneo, north and west of the Indonesian province of Kalimantan, consists of the former British colonies of Sarawak, North Borneo (Sabah), with Labuan and the Sultanate of Brunei. Sarawak and Labuan were created by James Brooke, the first 'White Raja' of Sarawak, and Sabah was founded by a London limited company. In 1946 Sarawak and Sabah become British colonies, and in 1963 joined the Malaysian Federation; Brunei chose to remain independent. Indonesia objected to the Federation and began a three-year period of low-intensity war, known as the *Konfrontasi*, successfully countered by British and Australian troops.

The cut and thrust of Hong Kong seemed a world away from the thick tropical jungle of Borneo that sweated beneath a steely sky. We adjusted to the heat in Sabah's capital, Kota Kinabalu. Flattened during the Second World War by Allied bombings, the small town was rebuilt in the 1950s on a tidy grid system that reminded us a little of Miami. Its busy main street is lined with tradition-al 'shophouses' – residential flats above shops. The markets are crowded and noisy, selling fruit and vegetables, herbs, spices, fish, chickens, basketware, orchids and ironmongery, and there are plenty of cafés and bars. After Kuala Lumpur, Kota Kinabalu is reputed to be the liveliest place in Malaysia. A couple of colonial buildings survived the bombings: the Atkinson clock tower, built in 1905 by the mother of the island's first district officer after he had died of malaria, and the old post office, now the Sabah Tourism Centre. On the way to the clock tower, we passed the town Padang where the British had held their first cricket match in 1901.

Borneo is the third largest island in the world and holds a strategic position in the middle of an important trading route between East and West. Once, it too was a trading focus for many nations, who exploited exotic jungle produce such as rhino horn, dammar resin, hornbill casques, kingfisher feathers and swifts' nests. When the British arrived they set up their first administrative centre on the large forested island Pulau Gaya, just off the coast and now part of the Tunku Abdul Rahman National Park, a marine reserve with clear seas rich in coral and brilliant tropical fish – a diver's dream. After the original settlement was destroyed by the local Bayan hero, Matt Salleh, the British relocated to the mainland fishing village of Api-Api (fire-fire), which expanded to become the capital Jesselton, renamed Kota Kinabalu in 1968 after nearby Mount Kinabalu.

∽ *A Promising Situation* ∽

The division of spoils between Spanish, Portuguese and Dutch in the East Indies had left Portugal with two small settlements on the mainland of India and China, Spain with the Philippines, and Holland with everything else, except the northern coast of Borneo and the Sulu archipelago. That region was claimed by two sultans, of Brunei and Sulu. Brunei had been in possession of all Borneo but surrendered the southern regions to the Dutch, which left the north-western coast, backed by the mountains that form the island's spine, from which many rivers flow into the South China Sea. The Sultan of Sulu, who ruled the small islands of the Sulu archipelago, the connecting link between the Philippines and the northern part of Brunei, was constantly occupied in fending off Spanish claims. For centuries Sulu and Brunei had engaged in shipping goods to China, Japan and India for Europe, even though the waters were infested with thousands of enterprising pirates, who hid on the islands or up the Bornean rivers.

It was only to be expected that, sooner or later, the British would decide to investigate this promising situation.

∼ An Idle Phantasy ∼

In 1760, the East India Company sent Alexander Dalrymple to establish a foothold in the area. He was an ambitious young Scotsman – later a contender for Cook's mission to New Zealand and Australia – and imagined carving out a new Polynesian empire. He took control of an island off the north coast of Borneo, but no one followed up his initiative: the Company was too busy with its new acquisitions in India to waste time in distant regions.

After the Napoleonic wars, ports were established at Singapore and Malacca, but neither the Company nor the British government wanted more responsibility and the pirates had not, as yet, interfered much with British trade.

John Crawfurd, the Company's agent in Singapore, dismissed Dalrymple's ideas as 'an idle phantasy . . . with respect to any country of Polynesia . . .' with the possible exception 'two or three centuries hence, of New Holland'.

Although Crawfurd's time-scale was wildly out, he was correct about the potential of the land that was becoming known as Australia.

∽ *Royalist's Invasion* ∽

In 1833 the East India Company surrendered its monopoly of British trade in the east, opening the field to its competitors. The first and most successful was Captain James Brooke, who had fought in the Company's army in Burma,

was invalided out, then inherited a modest fortune. An extravagantly romantic personality, he invested in an armed schooner, the *Royalist,* and sailed from Singapore to win 'a foothold from which the banner of civilisation could be unfurled, a task to which I would willingly devote my life, my energies, and my fortune'.

Royalist belonged to the Royal Yacht Squadron, and Brooke claimed that this 'admits her to the same privileges as a man-of-war':

The Byronically handsome Captain Brooke

he flew the white ensign to distinguish her from a vulgar merchantman – a mistake few would have made in the face of her half-dozen six-pounders. Brooke's considerable personal charm, allied to *Royalist*'s guns, convinced Sultan Musa, the Regent of Brunei, to hand over administration of the western tip of his province of Sarawak. Brooke and *Royalist*'s crew had founded a new state and the dynasty of Sarawak's white rajas.

∾ *Electric Intercourse* ∾

In London, James Brooke, a handsome and – intentionally – Byronic figure, fighting pirates and slavers, was a success and, as a respectable country gentleman untainted by trade, moved freely in official circles. However, the suspicion remained that his alter ego, the White Raja – the title had been made perpetual and hereditary after the first demonstration of his men's qualities – might commit some indiscretion that would embarrass Her Majesty's Government. The Admiralty welcomed an efficient ally in the fight against pirates, but the Foreign Office worried about clashes with other European powers. The Colonial Office was even less enthusiastic, concerned that yet more responsibility would be thrust upon it.

A compromise was reached in 1847 when Britain accepted the Sultan's offer of the tiny island of Labuan in Brunei Bay. It was too small – thirty-seven square miles – to be of great potential expense, and the Admiralty was pleased to find that it had a convenient seam of coal. Also, its position would serve well for what Brooke called 'electric intercourse', the submarine telegraph that was intended to link the British Empire. Brooke was appointed Labuan's first governor and awarded a knighthood. It was not a post that suited Sir James. As Raja, he enjoyed the cordial support of his

The Union Flag raised over the tiny colony of Labuan

people, who were delighted to be treated fairly and to join in punitive expeditions against the pirates; the Sultan acknowledged his value by extending his dominions, but Brooke was too impulsive and independent to put up with Colonial Office protocol.

∼ *The Richest Woman in England* ∼

Sarawak was only potentially rich: its main revenue came from the export of stibnite, the naturally occurring form of antimony that had been used widely as a cosmetic over millennia and was coming into demand as a metallic alloy. Unfortunately it generated too little income to cover the state's running expenses, much less to assist with development or expansion; in particular Brooke was desperate for an armed steamer to suppress piracy. No help was forthcoming from the British government. Instead, Brooke and Sarawak were rescued by the richest woman in England.

Angela Burdett-Coutts was the daughter of Radical MP Sir Francis Burdett, and heiress of the Coutts banking family's fortune. She was a close friend of the Duke of Wellington and the royal family, and knew almost everyone of note. She provided Brooke with enough funds for a gunboat, the *Rainbow*, but it took all her influence to persuade the British government to acknowledge Sarawak as an independent state, which it did in 1867. Sir James would have preferred Sarawak to be taken over as a Crown Colony, but the Colonial Office objected. It was 'just the old story – we are called upon to do an inconvenient and expensive thing because if we do not the French will . . .'

In 1879, two independently wealthy brothers, Alfred and Edward Dent, leased land from the Sultans of Brunei and Sulu, enabling them to establish the British North Borneo Company, mainly trading jungle produce with Singapore. Two years later they were granted a Royal Charter.

What had North Borneo been like when the British first arrived, we wondered. Kerry Tabrett has lived for many years on the island and is well versed in its history. 'The country was all jungle, completely undeveloped. When the

British arrived their first job was to clear out the pirates and stop the gun-running that went on.' There were around thirty-five different tribes, the most fearsome being the Kadazan head-hunters. Each of the tribes had different beliefs and ways of life. They were perpetually fighting and enslaving each other. The British planned to end the conflict, outlaw slavery, then plant coconut, tobacco and, later, rubber, bringing in Chinese labour to work the estates. 'Two of the strong things the British brought,' said Kerry, 'were the law and respect for peace, so people could begin to trade.'

∼ British North Borneo ∼

Frustrated at not having caught up with Britain in China, the French had turned their attention to South East Asia. In 1862 they had gained a foothold in Saigon, Vietnam, that had expanded within five years to cover all of the Mekong river basin. Northern Borneo and French Cochin China faced each other across the South China Sea, and the French navy minister exulted that his fleets could now 'put an end to all commercial relations between Singapore, Hong Kong and China and even menace India itself'. Once neglected, North Borneo, the province of Sabah, was now a source of worry to the British Foreign Office.

Brooke had an unquestioned lead south of Brunei, but the north was open for bids. The Dutch had always hoped to extend their territories, and the Italians were considering the establishment of a penal colony. The first action, however, was taken by an American, Joseph W. Torrey, who, in 1865, obtained a lease from the Sultan of Brunei. Since he failed to

HONG KONG

Ancient and modern.
A traditional junk in Victoria
Harbour, Hong Kong.

A chat with historian and
author Peter Moss in Hong
Kong Harbour.

Lamy Li gave me an intriguing
insight into the lives of Hong
Kong women.

Lee Hermie, the Hong Kong vet who has a lucrative practice treating the pampered pets of people too busy to have children.

William Ng shows me his moves. He's a Tai Chi master.

Strangely, the cat didn't crack a smile through the entire acupuncture session.

Locals praying at the Shinto Temple, a place of tranquility in the madness of Kowloon.

Incense being placed at the Shinto Temple in the heart of Kowloon.

Having my fortune told. Apparently I have a very long nose and very thin lips. I left there feeling like an ant-eater.

BORNEO

Downtown Kota Kinabalu.

The Clock Tower, the last British
building that remains in Sabah.

Kota Kinabalu night spot.

Agil, the descendent of a Head Hunter chief, and I on the bridge into his village, Monosopiad.

A collection of head-hunter's skulls in Monosopiad.

This stone, where the severed heads were displayed, still has a red stain running down it which I'm guessing is blood.

Wild Orchids were discovered in Borneo by Hugh Low.

An unexplained gap in the schedule for a breather.

That's the bird's nest they take the old bird spit out of.

This cave was full of rats and bat droppings and it stank. I loved it.

Just outside the caves of Gomantong where old swift nests are gathered to make the ludicrously expensive bird's nest soup.

I've adopted this one. She didn't seem very grateful.

Looking up into the forest, the natural habitat of the orang-utan.

One of our many airports – I have now devised a foolproof luggage check-in system. Details on application.

One of the many stunning tropical islands that sit off the coast of Borneo.

pay his rent the project was 'allowed to sleep', as the Foreign Office put it.

In 1878 when a British group offered to take over the administration of North Borneo from Torrey, the Foreign Office welcomed the idea as a convenient solution, but their Colonial Office colleagues were reluctant.

The moving spirit behind the new British North Borneo Company was Alfred Dent, a member of the Hong Kong family which had inadvertently precipitated the first Opium War. Lancelot Dent's successors had been incompetent, and by the 1860s the old family firm was bankrupt. Alfred, with his brother Edward, was determined to restore their fortunes; he had negotiated leases with the sultans of Sulu and Brunei and hoped to obtain a charter from the British government – an up-to-date version of the authority granted to the East India Company two hundred years previously. The Colonial Office was assured that Dent was 'a gentleman of the highest respectability', his group was 'purely British . . . have ample capital . . . and no idea whatever of parting with the concession to any foreigners or foreign state'.

The foreign threat came from Spain, which claimed Sulu and the adjacent coast of Sabah as part of the Philippines. In September 1878 a Spanish gunboat, with the Captain-General of the Philippines aboard, ordered the Spanish flag to be hoisted at one of the East India Company's settlements. The manager raised the Union flag and anchored his own ship across the Spanish line of fire. The Spanish retreated, but their aggression was 'calculated to cause very serious unease to Her Majesty's Government' and the Colonial Office was forced into a corner: 'Apparently we are to fight the Spaniards as well as the natives in order to put money into the pockets of these adventurers,' complained one official. The Foreign Secretary, Lord Salisbury had to step in, and concluded that the Dents must be given their charter.

We were curious as to who had come to Borneo, then a wild and distant island. 'They were mainly public-school boys who had decided to make a career out of administration,' Kerry told us. 'They got stuck into it and started ordering the natives around. It was pure force of character that made them take charge of an area.' Those maverick British men had even attempted to establish a telegraph system. 'That was difficult because they had to cut through virgin jungle with *parangs* [Malayan machetes]. When the line had been laid, it was hard to maintain, with trees falling down and elephants tearing it up. And when the natives found out about it they thought, "Aha, I'll take some of the wire for my wife's bangles". So the company had to change the brass wire for copper. But then the fellows thought, "This won't do for my wife but it'll do for making musket bullets."' The British also attempted to establish a one-metre gauge railway on the island, intended to join the west and east coasts, but that, too, was doomed to failure.

Kerry believed that those who came to Borneo made a completely different lifestyle from the one they had been used to at home. 'When the *mems* [women] came out they put on airs and graces. They had two or three servants whereas before they'd had none. Before independence in 1963, the relationship between the British and the locals was that of master and servant. The locals certainly weren't allowed in the club, and until then district officers were always British or European.'

～ *A Modest Success* ～

The white rajas' rule in Sarawak had been successful, but how would a London commercial company, quoted on the Stock Exchange, contrive to take over a wild territory about the size of Scotland and very much more rugged, even if the days of piracy were over? Under any circumstances it would have been hard, but in their anxiety to prove their good intentions the Dents nearly abandoned the concept of profitability. They promised 'free trade as far as possible', and that the 'rights of the natives' would be 'carefully guarded and provided for . . . every dollar

Tobacco was the first major commercial crop

raised by way of revenue or sales of land would be spent in the country'. They hoped to make a profit eventually from 'mining, cultivation, trading and so on', which was hardly a clear prospectus to attract investors.

Before cultivation could begin – tobacco was the first major commercial crop – land had to be cleared, and roads and wharves built. It was not until 1920 that the British North Borneo Company could begin operations with a

Any journey in the interior of Borneo was fraught with difficulty

logging company. In the meantime the main sources of revenue were the proceeds from land sales and whatever taxes the Dents could levy.

When Kerry decided to marry a Bornean woman, Teresa Sundang, the daughter of a native chief, the governor had warned him off, and his parents left the island with his brother. They didn't speak to him for thirty years. The rest of society ostracised him: 'I could only get a job in a timber company and I buried myself in the jungle for twenty years. I had made my bed and had to lie on it. My first two sons were treated as second-class citizens. We couldn't get an education for them here so I sent them to Australia to learn how to behave. My sons from my second marriage to Rose were born after independence and were treated quite differently.' Yet he never considered leaving the island. 'I love Borneo so I cut myself off and worked my way up until I was in management at the timber camp. I love the fact that it's warm here, unlike Margate where I came from. It's full of fascinating people and I'm fascinated by the history of the place. My life has been much more interesting than it would have been if I'd stayed in Britain.'

The Monosopiad Cultural Village, the only one of its kind in Sabah, is built where Monosopiad, a great Kadazan warrior, once lived. Today his descendants have built and manage this village, which aims to let visitors experience the Kadazans' way of life and to keep their culture alive. We crossed a rope bridge over a river that led into a clearing filled with native houses. Built of wood, bamboo and thatch, they stand on stilts so that neither rats nor water can get in and the airflow keeps the interior cool. In the centre of the village a large stone monolith, *Gintutun do Mohoing*, was once used for human sacrifice: the victim was tied to it and killed with bamboo spears. Tall bamboo poles surround it: the top of each is cup-shaped to hold a severed head as it dried in the open air. It is said that the stone is inhabited by spirits from the past.

We climbed steep wooden steps up to the longhouse of Agil Bajarai, the descendant of a head-hunter. It had been raining heavily when we arrived but inside it was completely dry. Large pots lined one wall and from the central roof beam forty-two skulls, darkened with age, were tied together with a natural twine, striking a macabre note. Outside a cock crowing or the clang of a gong broke the unnerving stillness in the house.

Agil is a tall, soft-spoken man, who immediately put us at ease. 'Head-hunters would take the head for its power,' he explained. 'They were taking the spirit of the person to use it as a blessing or to heal people. The more spirits you had the better, because then you could communicate with the next world. When you had someone's head, you automatically had everything else that belonged to him. We keep these heads to show the next generation so that they know their roots.'

Agil belongs to the Kadazan tribe, the largest indigenous group in Sabah. 'Sixty-five per cent of the population are Kadazan people. We have our own language but generally we speak Malay. When the British came they changed a lot. They brought a new language, schools, legal and administrative systems, and religion so that now ninety per cent of the people here are Christian. So we are grateful the British came here. Everybody still goes to the UK to study so there are a lot of ties. We watch the English Premier League here. Nobody wants to watch Italian or German football, only English!' Then he revealed that he is a Manchester United fan.

One of the island's early exports was sago, used in the eponymous pudding. It dawned on us that, although we had all eaten it, no one had the faintest idea where sago comes from. Agil took us to another clearing, by the river, where he pointed to a large split tree-trunk – part of a sago tree, from which the flesh is grated. 'We normally put all the flesh in that basket and step on it. The water will come away and we're left with the sediment. We put hot water on, stir it, and it becomes glue-like. We eat it like that.' That wasn't all the tree was good for: 'To get protein we eat the sago worm. We hold the head and eat the body. Sometimes we fry it first.'

Florence Kiloh-Stimol had married into a head-hunter family. She met us by the stone monolith. 'My grandparents lived in a British mission and my grandfather worked for the first European priest in the place I come from. The Kadazan are a loving people and welcomed the British, who brought education, religion and, by establishing a proper government, law and order.' The Kadazans' religion was similar in some ways to Christianity. They believe in a single god, but he has a wife and daughter. He is the Almighty, all-powerful, and created heaven and earth. They believe that after life on earth there will be another life exactly the same as this one, and that when someone dies, their spirit goes to the sacred Mount Kinabalu.

Although the impact of the British was largely positive, Florence believes that the Kadazan people are now losing their identity. 'Many of our young generation no longer know our native tongue and speak more English than Kadazan.'

To earn their Royal Charter, the British North Borneo Company had to show that they could make money in Borneo. Quelling the natives was time-consuming and the jungle lacked infrastructure, but there were unique treasures to be found – even if they weren't the money-spinners some had hoped for. A few decades earlier, Sir Hugh Low, a naturalist and colonial administrator based in Labuan, had climbed Mount Kinabalu three times, the first white man to reach its summit. He wrote about and drew what he found on the mountain's slopes. He was intrigued by the proliferation of orchids he discovered, some the size of pinheads and others with cascades of white flowers that were several metres long. To date, 480 different species have been named.

Victorian England became obsessed with orchids, so much so that a new word was coined – 'orchidelirium'. Orchid-collecting was a status symbol for the rich, although it was forbidden to women: the flowers were seen as too sexually suggestive, their name deriving from the Latin word 'orchis', meaning testicle. Nevertheless, Queen Victoria was an enthusiast and collector.

The swifts' nests that were essential in Chinese bird's nest soup were once an important source of income for the newly colonised country. Generally the British had been well-behaved in Borneo, but when they realised the value of the nest site, their negotiations with the local tribal leader to gain possession of Gomantong Caves deteriorated into fighting and he was killed.

On the long drive to the caves we saw that swathes of rainforest had been cleared for its timber and to make way for palm plantations. We passed mile after mile of them. The dusty roads reminded us of Ghana, and were dotted with wooden houses built on stilts. As we drove – slowly, because the side roads were considerably more potholed than anywhere we had been so far – groups of children buying coconut sweets waved to us from small stalls, the adults remaining under cover, shading themselves from the sun. Every now and then we overtook a large truck piled high with the red fruit of the oil palms.

Eventually we turned into the Gomantong Forest Reserve, arrived at the car park and made a short trek along a boardwalk. We were struck by the quiet of virgin rainforest. The leaves were so dense that we couldn't see far ahead, and it was plain that, off the boardwalk, you could easily get lost. The sharp contrast between this natural environment and the miles of palm trees brought home to us the tragedy of deforestation.

Before we saw the cave, we were hit by its acrid smell, which seeped everywhere on the breeze. A clearing had been made in the forest for long bamboo huts to house the workers who come here twice a year for a fortnight to collect the nests. A couple of men sat watching us silently, with coils of woven bamboo and rattan ladders beside them. Swifts darted in and out of the cave mouth as we went along the wooden perimeter walkway. High above us, barely visible in the thick vegetation covering the rock, there was a small wooden security post that guarded the treasure trove beneath.

In the centre of the cave, the floor was carpeted with swift and bat guano that seethed with golden cockroaches, crabs and beetles. In the dim light two small huts were barely visible, for the guards who watched over the nests twenty-four hours a day. The air was thick with particles of detritus and the overwhelming ammoniac stench of guano. We could think of no harder place to work. Flimsy rattan ladders, some 190 feet high, were suspended from the roof of the cave for the nest gatherers. There are two kinds of nest: those made with saliva and feathers, found here, and those made of pure saliva, found in nearby caves. Our guide explained how, after the feathers had been removed by hand, the nests are restored to their original cup shape, then sold.

Later, we were introduced to bird's nest soup by Tulip Noorazye, director of communications at the Tanjung Aru Hotel, who gave us a dish of bamboo pith, stuffed with bird's nest and topped with fried asparagus. 'This dish was reserved for the emperor, not for the common people,' she told us. 'The nests are very expensive. A kilo might cost as much as $3,500. The Chinese believe the bird's nest offers nutritional and medicinal benefits. It's good for the common cold, coughs and asthma. They say it rejuvenates you, is good for your skin and for pregnant ladies because it helps babies have strong lungs. The nest itself doesn't have any taste, which is why we serve it in soup or with a sauce.' Dishes including birds' nests are produced on special occasions to show off a host's wealth.

The last place on our itinerary was at the edge of more virgin rainforest: the Sepilok Rehabilitation Centre for orang-utans. Borneo is one of the few places that is still home to a creature that had a fundamental impact not only on Victorian Britain but on the world's thinking. In 1838, Charles Darwin saw his first primate – an orang-utan named Jenny, in London Zoo. He was astonished by how human she looked – which led to his first thoughts on human evolution, then a theory that caused a storm in Christian Victorian Britain. That man should be descended from an ape was absurd. Indeed, when Queen Victoria saw a second orang-utan at the zoo and 'took tea with it', she commented that it was 'frightful, and painfully and disagreeably human'.

A short drive from the old island capital of Sandakan, the orang-utan centre was founded in 1964 on the edge of the Kabili Sepilok Forest Reserve. Sepilok was set up after the British introduced the timber trade to the island. Initially 'clear felling' meant that an area was completely cleared, which simultaneously destroyed the indigenous wildlife. The British soon grasped the devastation that this was causing, which led to the foundation of the first forest reserves in Sabah. Today, the Sabah Wildlife Department works hard to preserve these precious species, not least for their appeal to tourists. The government is also trying to ensure that logging is done sustainably so the animals have a chance to move deeper into the forest. Now Sabah Wildlife protect the orang-utan with the help of the Sepilok Orang-utan Appeal, a British-based charity set up by Sue Sheward, who raises money for the animals through an adoption scheme.

Dr Sen Nathan, chief wildlife vet at Sabah Wildlife Department, introduced us to orphaned orang-utans. 'If a tree needs to be felled in the process of land clearing, a mother orang-utan may be high up a tree when it is cut without the logger realising. The tree is cut, the mother falls, breaks the fall of the young ones and dies. Sometimes the young are kept as pets by the workers – loggers or those converting the land for agriculture – or they are handed over to Sabah Wildlife and brought here. Sabah Wildlife has an enforcement unit. We have teams that act on tip-offs and collect baby orang-utans that have been kept as pets. It's illegal to keep them as pets here, and if you are caught, there's a mandatory six-month jail sentence and a hefty fine.'

Often when the animals arrive, they have to be retrained to eat the appropriate diet. Sen told us of a childless Indonesian couple, estate workers on an oil-palm plantation, who 'kept a baby orang-utan for three years. They dressed and fed him as a baby. When we went to get him, they didn't want to let him go. But when we explained they might go to jail, they understood that they had to.'

After two years in the centre's indoor nursery, where they learn everything their mother would have taught them, such as how to climb, they are taken to the outdoor nursery. 'This is their first experience of the forest world. We have a few feeding platforms so that we can feed them further and further into the forest. Some come here when they're five or six, and by the time they're seven or eight they're totally independent. Others stay close to the centre until they're ten or twelve.'

The nursery is at the top of a steep hill three or four minutes' walk further into the rainforest. Steep concrete steps lead to a couple of large cages and the orang-utans were playing over and around them, but never inside. We were told not to touch the animals as they walked round us, which meant they could do whatever they liked to us until the attendants prised them away.

Sheena Hynd, a primatologist whose ground-breaking research is funded by the Sepilok Orang-utan Appeal, took us round the outdoor training area, introducing the orang-utans by name. 'In the wild, they live until their late thirties,' she said, 'so hopefully these have a long life ahead. When they're first released they go into a large enclosure for about a week to get used to being out at night and to having the older ones around. Then they're released and fed on the different feeding plat-forms.' She pointed out a couple that were stationed on the edge of the forest with long ropes swinging above them that disappeared into the forest. 'When they're comfortable in the area, they disperse into the forest. There are other feeding platforms further in where they can come for food twice a day. Eventually they stop coming and become fully independent, although some-times they pop back for a couple of weeks to make sure everything's OK here.'

They live too high in the forest canopy for any predator to be a threat. 'If they're down here, we have had instances when juvenile orang-utans have been victims of a clouded leopard – even in Sepilok. But up there in the forest, they are totally safe.' Fully grown adult males can weigh up to a hundred and fifty kilos, and the females about half that. 'The female will start having babies when she's between eight and ten. The gestation period is nine months, like humans, and once she has had the baby, it stays with her for four or five years. That's when she will try to wean it, and that's probably when she's trying to get naughty again. If she lives to a ripe old age, she might have four to six babies in her lifetime.'

Once the animals have been rehabilitated, the centre has no way of knowing what happens to them. 'They have identichips and three numbers tattooed on their leg so you can identify them if they return here,' explained Sheena, 'but you can't track them. All we can do is follow them on foot, observing them to see how they get on.' If they return to the centre, they aren't always recognisable. 'They change immensely, especially the big males, who start getting their cheek pads, phalanges, which make their face moon-shaped.' We were impressed by the dedication of the staff at Sepilok and before we left the jungle we decided, with the help of Kristina Maurice-Jones of the Sepilok Orang-utan Appeal, to adopt a cheeky little ape we had seen earlier in the day, in the hope that this might help secure a brighter future for her.

∾ *Occupation and Resistance* ∾

Borneo was devastated by the Japanese invasion in January 1942. After a prolonged and courageous resistance by the Indian Army's Punjabis, with British gunners and Engineers, a local resistance movement was established, led by Tom Harrisson of the Special Operations Executive. Apart from James Brooke, Harrisson was the most colourful and distinguished man in Bornean history, an anthropologist, founder of Mass Observation – the pioneer social-research organisation – and a successful resistance fighter. With the enthusiastic support of the populace, Harrisson and his men demoralised the Japanese forces in many conflicts and re-established control of several areas.

Sabah also witnessed one of the most terrible demonstrations of Japanese military brutality in the Sandakan prison camp and in the forced march from there to the interior. Of more than six thousand prisoners-of-war only three survived to describe their ordeal, and ensure the execution of the camp commanders.

General MacArthur accepts the Japanese surrender

∼ Post-War Reconstruction ∼

Japanese destruction and Allied bombardment had so devastated the infrastructure that neither the Brooke family nor the North Borneo Company could shoulder the costs of reconstruction, so in June 1946 the Colonial Office took over in North and South Borneo.

From the investors' point of view, the results were disappointing: the Dents had failed to restore or augment their family fortune. When the territory reverted to the Crown the shareholders received ten shillings in the pound, which just exceeded the highest price they had ever seen on the market.

Dent's administration was capable and honest, if unin-spiring, but its profits were meagre. To London sharehold-ers, reputation was less important than dividends, and in 1894 dissident investors appointed W. C. Cowie as manag-ing director, instructing him to produce profits by any means he wished. Sir Lester Paul Beaufort, grandson of a Hong Kong governor, was recruited to assist him, but he was ignorant of trade and the East. Despite that, in 1895 he became governor of North Borneo and Labuan. Alfred Dent resigned in disgust, and between them Cowie and Beaufort nearly ruined North Borneo. Grandiose projects – the tele-graph line from Labuan and the railway from Brunei – were put in hand, financed by raised taxes.

A tax on rice, the staple food, was deeply resented, and led to a serious rebellion against the British North Borneo Company's rule: the Matt Salleh revolt. In the subdued style of the North Borneo government, the rebellion was a mod-erate affair and began with protests from Datu Muhammad Salleh – Matt Salleh – an independent local magnate, against Company interference. When he and Cowie met, they reached agreement on how to move forward, but their sup-porters were infuriated. Fighting broke out again, and only ended with Matt Salleh's death in 1900. The railway's route had to be shortened, but a line was opened in 1902, partly funded by the Company's income from its monopoly on opium imports.

However, they left a peaceful and modestly profitable community, with an adequate infrastructure and an unspoiled environment: ruthless logging had not destroyed the forests, and wildlife flourished. Many professionally administered colonies did not do as well.

When it was suggested that Borneo should join the new Malaysian Federation, Indonesia objected violently, and began their *Konfrontasi*, or campaign of violent infiltration. The federation was formally inaugurated in September 1963, but British and Australian troops fought for two more years before Indonesia backed down.

The new administration has not fulfilled Dent's early hopes. By 2002 the rainforest had been largely destroyed, and in 2006 it was reported that the government was about to permit logging in previously protected areas. A London commercial company, with all its disadvantages, had served the environment better.

Borneo still seems an outpost, fighting to preserve tolerance in an increasingly intolerant world, where fundamentalism would like to reign. In the lush park below Mount Kinabalu's Victoria Peak, we were taken aback to hear one park guide call some of the first British settlers, Sabah's 'first pioneers', the men who catalogued and attempted to understand his homeland's glorious natural history. To others in Sabah the British brought peace, education and administration allowing a previously tribal country to enter a world stage, yet they introduced with it a system riddled with racism. Just as in the other places we visited, the British arrived and made a definite mark.

7

New Zealand

This was the start of our real glory days. Sorry, I'm not talking about the Empire, I mean our new luggage-numbering system. I'd introduced a radical new counting scheme round about Hong Kong or Borneo. It was bold but simple. Hand luggage would go on its own trolley. And it would be put to one side, minded by Isabel, our makeup artist, and would form no part of our calculations. As the gear came off the belt, it was to be stacked on trolleys in increments of five – five items, no more, no less, to be on each trolley. Once a trolley had its quota, it was to be lined up with the others and from then on, only trolleys would need to be counted, not individual items.

There were some luggage Luddites who still swore by the let's-put-it-in-a-long-line-and-get-in-everyone's-way approach, and although I knew I was right, I had to back down in case they left me out of focus. But in the short evenings between a long day's filming and a ludicrously crack-of-dawn departure, we swore that one day we would have labels, and numbers, and a big list and, lo, it came to pass and there was no more counting or slapping, just cheerful ticking and calm checking and we were happy.

We left for Auckland on a Friday and by Sunday I'd run out of things to read and we were still flying. I had to watch a ludicrous movie with Demi Moore where she went to live in the Scottish Highlands, arriving with one tiny suitcase but wearing a different huge coat in every scene. Perhaps she had them delivered – like milk. Instead of a milk float, a coat float.

We flew up to the Bay of Islands the day we arrived in Auckland. It was a tiny very noisy plane and I had a yelled conversation with a farmer in the next seat. I told him about our programme – I really wanted to tell him about our luggage-numbering system but the others were frowning and mouthing "Don't mention the luggage," so we talked about the Empire. I asked him what he thought the main consequence was of the British taking over New Zealand. He didn't hesitate. "Gorse." Beg pardon? "Gorse". You know, the prickly yellow stuff. We brought it and now they can't get rid of it.

The Bay of Islands is gorgeous. It's like a bigger, better, cleaner, more spectacular Lake District, but I could never forget how far I was from home. I couldn't imagine having the courage to up sticks as so many did two hundred years ago, and set sail from England to make a new life. At least I could text my children – I didn't have to wait six months for a letter. No, I'd have to wait six months for a text.

∾ Introduction ∾

The world's youngest country in terms of population, New Zealand was first settled by the Maori, probably about seven centuries ago. When British colonists in Australia and visiting whalers began to trade with them in the early nineteenth century, missionaries and the colonial authorities insisted on a formal agreement between the incoming Pakeha, as the Maori called the British, and the Maori themselves. The Treaty of Waitangi was signed in 1840, but a series of wars took place in the following years. By 1870 New Zealand was self-governing, with the Maori holding a special position in the constitution, with their own monarch.

After the development of refrigerated shipping, exports of meat and dairy products have underpinned New Zealand's prosperity; more recently tourism has become a major industry, stimulated by its magnificent scenery. In the United Nations' assessment of development, New Zealand ranks between Germany and Italy as one of the world's most advanced societies – and remains a monarchy.

The glittering waters of the Pacific Ocean stretch away from the northern tip of the north-east coast of New Zealand, interrupted by one hundred and forty-four tree-covered rocky islands. Under the bluest of skies a shoal of dolphins leaps clear of the translucent aquamarine water. This is the Bay of Islands, some of the most glorious scenery we'd seen so far. Aboard the car ferry taking us across the bay from Opua to Russell, we could see white clapboard houses dotted along the shoreline. We had been drawn to New Zealand by tales of Captain Cook who, on his way to Australia, had landed here in 1769, attracted by the natural harbour and whaling stories.

∼ *The Most Effective Predators* ∼

Some time during the thirteenth century a couple of hundred adventurers made their way to New Zealand, which is nearly two thousand miles from eastern Polynesia. They were descendants of the Island Polynesians who, in previous millennia, had populated much of the Pacific. We know that they came from the east, rather than the nearer (but still a thousand miles away) western islands, such as Tonga, because they brought with them, among many other plants, the sweet potato, a South American vegetable.

The Maori's ancestors found a land swarming with food: fish, seals and moa, the great flightless bird, were there for the catching. Although the first settlers were dependent on stone or bone tools and weapons, they slaughtered seals and had cleared the land of moa within a couple of centuries: humans are the most effective predators.

The now-extinct moa could measure 12 feet in height

Left to themselves, the Maori evolved a complex culture, not only of aristocrats and commoners, but of the gifted: craftsmen, such as carvers, bards and hunters were much respected. An individual's 'mana' or authority, inherited or acquired, was the ultimate measure of his self-respect and standing in the community.

The Maori's first contact with the outside world was short and violent. In December 1642 Captain Abel Janszoon Tasman, of the Dutch East India Company, anchored off the northern tip of the South Island in what he called Murderers Bay. Maori attacked one of the ship's boats and killed four seamen. One body was taken ashore – 'the first of many European imports consumed in New Zealand,' commented an eminent New Zealand historian.

The next European visitors, and the first to set foot in New Zealand, were the crew of Captain James Cook's ship, *Endeavour*. In October 1769, having sailed to Tahiti to observe the transit of Venus across the sun with the distinguished naturalists Joseph Banks and Daniel Solander, Cook went south to discover whether or not the great continent that was thought to lie between Australia and South America actually existed. Alexander Dalrymple, who founded the first British settlement in Borneo, insisted that a great landmass was waiting, with a population of fifty million, to be incorporated into the British Empire. Instead, Cook circumnavigated what Tasman had called Nieuw Zeeland, and charted its coastline.

Cook had been told to treat the natives with respect. 'No European nation has the right to occupy any part of their country . . . without their voluntary consent.' But he hardly needed the warning. Many years later, a Maori boy recalled him: 'There was one supreme man in that ship. We knew that he was lord of the whole by his very perfect and gentlemanly demeanour . . . He was a very good man and came to us – the children – and patted our cheeks and gently touched our heads.' The encounters were not always friendly: a ritual emerged of challenge and response, followed by an armed clash. *Endeavour*'s crew attempted to inflict as little harm as possible, and Banks noted that 'always after one night's consideration they have observed our superiority but hardly before'. Once the peaceful intentions of the British were understood, subsequent relations were usually amicable: '. . . no one shewed the least signs of fear . . .' and the girls were 'as great coquetts as any Europeans could be . . .'

Captain Cook: 'a very good man'

It is hard to believe now that the vibrant, well-heeled community of Russell was once known as the 'Hell Hole of the Pacific'. Originally named Kokorareka ('sweet blue penguin'), it was one of the first European settlements in New Zealand, established during the early nineteenth century. Whaling ships stopped there to trade guns and alcohol with the indigenous Maori, who provided them with timber and food in return. A lawless community grew up, inviting an influx of missionaries, who did their best to restore some measure of morality.

Today Russell is a peaceful place where out-of-towners have holiday homes, and several historic buildings still stand: the Pompallier Mission, built in 1842 as a printing works by the Catholic mission; Christ Church, the oldest church in New Zealand, which dates back to 1836; the weatherboard police station with its picket fence; and the Duke of Marlborough Hotel. Oyster-farming, fishing, crafts and tourism are the town's main sources of income, and a long jetty leads out to sea.

Russell was gearing up for the tourist season when we arrived and felt as if it was waking from a long sleep. The summer sun was beginning to bake the quiet streets of white houses with red or grey tiled roofs, but a wintry breeze was blowing.

∼ Muskets, Missionaries and Mutineers ∼

Once the British government, prompted by Joseph Banks, had decided to site a convict colony at Botany Bay, in Australia, and the First Fleet of convict transports had disembarked in January 1788, it was not long before their attention turned to New Zealand. Other than deserters from visiting ships, the first Australians to arrive were sealers, who, like the Maori before them, had soon exterminated the fur-seal colonies. British and American whalers followed – Herman Melville's tattooed harpooner in *Moby Dick*, Queequeg, was probably based on a Maori – using the Bay of Islands as a home port.

Charles Darwin, who called in during the *Beagle's* famous voyage, referred to the British there as 'the refuse of society'.

One resident was Charlotte Badger, an enterprising girl who in 1806, en route between Sydney and Hobart where she had been sentenced for picking pockets, contrived with another girl to seduce the mate of their aptly named transport, the *Venus*. After a successful mutiny, the three began a joint career as pirates until they arrived in the Bay of Islands. There, Charlotte lived with a Maori chief and eventually took off with an American whaling captain.

Traders coming from New South Wales to buy flax for naval canvas found a ready market for cheap, reliable muskets. Maori communities had always been belligerent, but had avoided excessive casualties, with their well-understood ritual of challenge and defiance, and the limitations imposed by their weapons. But firearms introduced a new scale of deadliness. A recent historian wrote, 'If any chapter of New Zealand history has earned the label 'holocaust' it was the Musket Wars . . . ' These ensued as tribes fought for supremacy: perhaps twenty per cent of the Maori were wiped out during the twenty years of the wars, which were routinely accompanied by torture, enslavement and cannibalism. By 1830, the price of muskets, which had been eight pigs and ten stones of potatoes, had fallen to a couple of smoked heads; slaves ensured a constant supply.

In Australian histories the Reverend Samuel Marsden, Anglican chaplain and magistrate to the colony of New South Wales, is usually condemned as the 'flogging parson', more concerned with personal profit and keeping convicts subdued in his capacity as magistrate than with their spiritual needs. In New Zealand he is a revered founding father. Both assessments are substantially correct. A blunt, impatient Yorkshireman, Marsden was a committed evangelical, but

Samuel Marsden (centre) met by Maori: 'a very superior people'

had little interest in ministering to Aborigines because 'they have no Reflection', preferring to concentrate on the Maori: 'a very superior people in point of mental capacity'. Between his first sermon, given on Christmas Day 1814, and his last visit, in 1837, Marsden made seven voyages across the Tasman Sea, at his own expense, and founded seven mission stations.

With evangelism went literacy, stimulated by a translation of the scriptures into Maori, which was published by the Church Missionary Society from 1835. Between 1809 and 1821, Marsden welcomed more than a hundred to his extensive farm at Parramatta, New South Wales, which became almost a 'great Maori college of European studies'. Largely as a result of his work, Maori were able to meet the 'shock of the new', the challenge of British colonisation, on more equal terms. Muskets and military skills helped, but in the long run they could not protect Maori rights and culture.

James Belich is a leading historian at the University of Auckland. Sitting on a bench overlooking the water at Russell, shaded by some of the huge non-indigenous European trees that have been there for almost a hundred and fifty years, he told us what had happened when the British first arrived in New Zealand. As he talked, the sea lapped on the pebbly beach, about thirty feet from the grass where we were sitting.

'The whalers were from all nations – French, a few Danish and Dutch, Australians, but mainly British and Americans. I'm afraid wherever you've got thousands of sailors you tend to have the same story. It probably wasn't a hell of a lot worse than in other places but the missionaries tended to exaggerate it.' He went on to describe those who tried to convert the Maori to Christianity and European civilisation. 'They tended to think the two were the same thing. They had the arrogance and racial preconceptions of their time but they were altruistic too. I think they deserve a certain amount of respect, but you can't trust their record because they saw everything through their rather puritanical, evangelical lenses.

'To begin with, the Maori and the missionaries got on well. The Maori were converted but they bent Christianity their way and incorporated some of their own rituals and concepts. Both sides felt they were achieving different things, yet it worked.' If not for long. 'The missionary love affair with the Maori lasted until 1860 when it all turned to custard with a major conflict between the British and the Maori when the benign illusion that both the Maori and the British were in charge was punctured. Specific factors included the scale of British immigration, which had shifted up several gears during the 1850s. The Maori could handle hundreds or even thousands of British settlers, but when tens and even hundreds of thousands came, more pressure was put on the Maori relationship than it could stand. Also the British expected to have the upper hand when they were in partnership with a non-European people, to whom they considered themselves superior. When they found that they didn't, all hell broke loose.'

The Maori were a substantial force, armed with muskets and cannons that they'd traded from the whalers. 'However, they had a problem with their ammunition supply. They couldn't get the proper round shot so they tended to use bullock chain in the cannons. Their artillery wasn't particularly successful but they put up a good fight, and it was only when the imperial government applied no less than twelve thousand soldiers, plus a lot of colonial troops, that they were able to curb the independence of the Maori tribes in the 1860s.'

Why had there been such an influx of Britons at that time. 'They saw New Zealand as a potentially better Britain. They'd been told that it was a place where they'd earn better wages, where they could acquire their own freehold land, where they'd be treated with respect. The letters sent home by settlers would tell them, 'You're going to get prime meat three times a day instead of scrag end. You'll be able to hunt instead of being arrested for poaching. You'll be able to ride a horse instead of relying on shanks's pony. You'll be able to have holidays, own a house. There'll be bosses but you won't have to call them 'sir' and you won't have to doff your cap." The appearance at least of egalitarianism was very attractive to mid-nineteenth-century British common folk.'

Were they threatened or frightened by the idea of the Maori? 'They were told that the Maori were dying out, that they loved the British and were rapidly being civilised into brown Britons, and that they weren't all over the country anyway.'

The settlers found that New Zealand was good for sheep so they sold wool to the British textile mills. Eventually they found gold, too. 'Their sheer numbers created a domestic market that enabled New Zealand to develop through its own growth. In 1840, there were less than a thousand Europeans in New Zealand. By the early 1880s – a single lifetime later – there were half a million.'

In 1840 the British and the Maori had signed the Treaty of Waitangi. It was intended to secure a peace but it became the source of terrible misunderstanding. What happened? 'The key is that there were two versions of the treaty,' James explained. 'The Maori version said that the British would run their own settlers and the Maori would run themselves; the English-language version said that the British would run both. That misunderstanding was eventually the cause of the wars. For about twenty years the Maori version dominated, but then the New Zealand wars broke out and persisted until 1872. They turned the tide against Maori independence and the British version became reality from about 1870.

'From around 1970, there was a resurgence of interest in the treaty and in Maori activism. Maori came to see the treaty as a covenant that offered some sort of protection of their place in New Zealand. Since then, although the idea of a new constitution is occasionally broached, the Maori version of the treaty has become something of a sacred document that's somehow the essence of New Zealand. It's not that common to have a treaty of this kind between two peoples.'

∾ The Treaty of Waitangi ∾

The enthusiasm for colonisation, which formed in the 1830s, focused first on New South Wales, Australia, but soon spread to New Zealand. Free from any convict problems, with a climate similar to Britain's, it was surely an ideal destination. The Colonial Office insisted that, as Cook had been warned seventy years previously, agreement with the Maori was essential, and that this should be formally recorded: the Maori were well organised, well armed, and capable of defending their rights. Many of their leaders were literate, too, and accustomed to debate with the Pakeha, as the British were known.

Governor George Gipps of New South Wales was all too conscious of the devastating effects of settler greed on the Australian Aborigines, and was determined to protect Maori interests. The Treaty of Waitangi, agreed in a four-day meeting in February 1840, was the result. The British party was headed by Captain William Hobson RN, who had already spent time in both Australia and New Zealand. In the absence of wars, nineteenth-century naval officers were expected to turn their hands to anything. With the assistance of his secretary, a handful of missionaries and eleven alcohol-ridden New South Wales police troopers, Hobson had to agree what would become the cornerstone of a constitution that would protect Maori rights and allow for British colonisation in a country rather larger than Great Britain.

Hobson drafted an English version, which was translated overnight into Maori. On 5 February copies were distributed and read to Maori chiefs and people – hundreds had gathered in a vast marquee. They debated it for the rest of the day and through the night, and the treaty was signed on 6 February. More discussion and signing took place across New Zealand, and on 21 May 1840 Hobson declared British sovereignty over the entire country – stimulated, once again, by news that the French were planning a settlement on the South Island.

It was hardly surprising that the treaty was flawed; rather, it is amazing that it worked as well as it has. Apart from the transfer of sovereignty to Great Britain, its most essential clause was that which guaranteed 'full, exclusive and undisturbed possession of all Maori lands' until they wished to sell, and sales could only be made to the government, which could sell on or grant them as it wished. It should have been obvious that, without a definition of 'Maori lands', clashes with land-hungry colonists were inevitable.

In 1839 the unscrupulous and influential Wakefield brothers, Edward Gibbon and Arthur, both of whom had served time for the attempted abduction of a young heiress, had succeeded, against the opposition of the Colonial Office, in establishing the New Zealand Land Company. The way was now open for an influx of settlers from Britain: Edward encouraged them with optimistic promises in London, while in New Zealand Arthur arranged land transfers with no regard for Maori traditions or the treaty, which the Company regarded as no more than 'a praiseworthy device for amusing and pacifying savages for the moment'.

Robert Fitzroy, who had been Darwin's captain on the *Beagle* and succeeded Hobson as Governor floundered in an impossible position between treaty promises and settler greed. One deal cost Arthur Wakefield his life. He attempted to eject Maori from land he claimed illegally to own; it was his own fault, Governor Fitzroy considered, but his act led to the first Maori War.

After we were told that dolphins had been sighted in the bay, we hired a boat to go and find them. Inland, Northland looks like the Cotswolds or Derbyshire on a grand scale, but from the ocean the volcanic islands and cliff edges were reminiscent of the landscape we had glimpsed when the sun came out in Newfoundland.

A little way from shore we found a pod of forty or fifty dolphins, which swam alongside the boat, leaping and playing with us. Our boatman worked with them every season when they passed through, so he knew their behaviour. He would navigate one way, spin round and go back through the wake, knowing that when they're in the right mood dolphins love to leap five or six feet out of the water; that they swam along in the wake of the boat

NEW ZEALAND

The Bay of Islands – like a bigger, cleaner, emptier Lake District.

A playful dolphin plays catch up with us in the Bay of Islands.

Russell Police Station and the Great Marlborough Pub in Russell, the first European settlement in New Zealand and a town known as 'The Hellhole of the Pacific'.

Greeting Hone in the traditional Maori fashion. I think the reason his hair looks so good is that the water is pure. Long way to go for a shampoo, though!

Hone takes a break from us filming him and his people in their 'waka'.
Hone's chanting keeps time as the rowers row.

A Maori carving on the Waitangi Treaty Grounds.

The flagpole on the grounds where a controversial treaty was signed between the British and Maori leaders.

Looking at these graves made me very aware of the tenacity and courage of the Scottish settlers who came so far from home for the sake of their religion.

It's like the Derby
Dales with giant ferns!

Colonial architecture is dotted all around New Zealand's
largest city, Auckland.

Sylvia and Leicester Martin. He proposed to her while he was in the RAF during the Second World War, so she came to New Zealand as a nervous war bride.

Willie Jackson and Lindsay Perigo in the middle of an acrimonious debate about Maori land rights. There's no point showing me because I couldn't get a word in.

because they enjoy human company. As they leapt and turned in the water, one of us would catch a twinkling dolphin eye and experience a moment of connection.

Our assistant cameraman told us about a holiday-maker who had mistaken a dolphin for a shark, when it nudged his wife's hand, which was dangling in the water. He had shot it, and a local boatman saw the incident. Within a couple of hours, word had spread and a hundred furious local people were baying for the couple's blood. A police escort had to helicopter them safely out of the area.

The intricately carved white prow of the *waka*, a long Maori canoe, cut through the water, paddled by around twenty Maori men and women in traditional dress. The men wore fringed loincloths, some with tattoos that covered most of their bodies while the women were dressed more modestly. They sat in pairs with a steersman in the stern and a small child kneeling on the prow. The leader stood in the centre of the boat, chanting. His chest and shoulders were tattooed and a traditional Maori carved-bone fishhook hung on a necklace. The chant had the dual purpose of instructing the paddling and reiterating the ancestors' epic journey from Polynesia to New Zealand, and we were transported into the past.

We had been filming around the cool, windy bay for nearly an hour when we became concerned that the crew of the *waka* must be exhausted, and brought out tea and biscuits. We asked them to join us, and discovered a staunch traditionalist among them who tried to stop the others taking a chocolate-chip cookie. He told his colleagues to give them back, but a few of the women ate them, pretending they hadn't heard! Later, back on land, they performed a traditional Maori *haka* for us. It is a complex and alarming short dance, in which hands, arms, legs, voice, tongue and eyes play a part, and can be seen in a modified version at every All Black rugby match. We wanted to film them against the setting sun but they ignored us. We soon realised they had to adopt set positions and that we were trying to force them into doing something that wasn't true to their tradition.

James had told us about early misunderstandings between the Maori and the British. 'The Maori performed their welcoming *haka* while the Europeans did their twenty-one-gun salute and a display of marines marching up the beach. Both misunderstood the other's encounter rituals for aggression, so there was conflict. But once they learnt to communicate, the phase of co-operation lasted until the 1860s.' Today, such Maori rituals are performed regularly to keep alive the culture that many Maori feel is in danger of being lost. Now it came as a shock to us when the *waka* crew changed into western-style clothes and climbed into their 4x4s to drive back to their contemporary life.

Their leader was Hone Mihaka, who had volunteered to meet us at Waitangi to talk to us about the treaty from the Maori point of view. The following morning we walked through the forest behind our hotel and up to a grassy promontory looking across the water to Russell. The one-storey Georgian colonial-style Treaty House, built for the first British resident, Sir James Busby, is a simple building, apparently because the necessary materials for something grander weren't delivered from Sydney. In front of it a flagpole marks the spot where the agreement was signed. Nearby *Te Whare Runanga*, a carved Maori meeting-house, was built a hundred years later, and *Ngatokimatawhaorua*, the largest Maori war canoe, is preserved in a special boathouse. We sat with Hone on some rocks just below the flagpole, overlooking the water where he had captained the *waka* the day before, and asked about his ancestors.

'In my genealogy we don't come from another land,' he explained. 'My father told me that our ancestors were here when the first Maori arrived a thousand years ago and Kupe [a Polynesian leader] was brought on the fingertips of the guardian of the wind. Our ancestors stood here and watched the arrival of the first *waka*. Many other races have visited these islands since the beginning of time. Every time they have come here we have been here to welcome them and invite them to be friends with our people.'

The Maori believe they have an indissoluble spiritual link with the land. 'My DNA reading is the same as the DNA of the land. We are one,' Hone explained.

How had his ancestors lived before the arrival of the Europeans? 'They were fishermen and agriculturalists. They worked the forest, the land and the sea. They grew sweet potato and corn, and hunted different types of birds – pigeon, tui, kiwi – and rats in the forest.' The arrival of Europeans had opened up worldwide trading opportunities for the Maori, who until then had been trading only across the Pacific. 'It was win-win for both of them until the Treaty of Waitangi. The original text was written in what is known today as the Maori language. The missionaries listened to the words of my ancestors and wrote the words using an English phonetic alphabet, but when the

words were translated, the true meaning and the true spir-
ituality of the Treaty of Waitangi were lost for ever.'

We wanted him to tell us what the words had meant
before they were translated into English. 'Given I have a
partial academic background, my understanding of what
our ancestors were trying to do is that they wanted to
open a trade route. It was an agreement to trade equally
and fairly with each other.' However, because Kororareka
was a lawless settlement, it had a second purpose: 'It was
also an invitation to Queen Victoria, the chief of all white
people, to come here and govern, watch over those
thieves, murderers and others who were creating havoc
here. The British interpretation was that our people would
hand over all sovereignty to the Queen: it was a land and
sea-devouring dragon that came and ate up all our land
and resources.' Hone paused. 'For some reason, the
British thought we really needed them to look after us, but
we had done a marvellous job of looking after ourselves
for millions of years, long before our first contact with
Europeans. Today we feel as we did then that the British
and Europeans who come here need to be looked after by
us. To us, they will always be esteemed guests.'

Despite the problems of the past, Hone has a clear
vision of New Zealand's future: 'I would like all things to
be equal: people enjoying each other, enjoying living with
each other and benefiting from each other. That's how I
see the future. It may take us another hundred and fifty
years to get back to the top in terms of an economic and
social scale, but inside we will always be at the top.'

As we ended our conversation, he took a small bone out
of his ear-lobe that decorated and stretched it. He blew

through it, as his father had taught him, to produce a melancholy tune. Out to sea, the early-morning sky was overcast and misty as the sun tried to burst through.

As we left, three flags caught our attention: the Union flag, the New Zealand flag and the flag of the united tribes. We commented on how similar the latter was to the Union flag. It features the St George Cross, the top left-hand corner filled with four white stars on a deep blue background separated by a red cross with a white outline, and we asked Hone if the Maoris were happy with it. 'Are you joking?' He was astounded. 'That is the flag our fore-fathers chose and we're very happy with it.'

∽ George Grey ∽

Sir George Grey was the most talented and experienced colonial leader of the nineteenth century. Polymath, author, founder of the magnificent Grey Library in Cape Town and the Maori Collection in Auckland, explorer – shipwrecked and wounded by Australian Aborigines – soldier, Governor of South Australia and of New Zealand (twice), High Commissioner of South Africa, Prime Minister of New Zealand and a founding member of the Australian Labor Party, he was also an autocrat, convinced (as dictators always are) of his own infallibility. Quite often he was right.

Grey's first period of office, from 1845 to 1853, initiated a period of calm interaction between Maori and British. The first Maori War had not gone well for the British, since the opposing forces were evenly matched; both were armed with the basic infantry smoothbore musket, and the Maori were able to shelter in well-fortified 'pahs' surrounded by entrenchments and firing pits. Grey ended the fighting and gained acceptance by the Maori as a sort of paramount chief, having learnt their language and their traditions of negotiation.

He matched conciliation of the Maori with firm treatment of the settlers: he refused to implement a draft constitution sent out by the Colonial Office on the grounds that it would give the latter too much power, and prepared his own version, which became New Zealand's first representative constitution.

In 1858, his successor, Colonel Gore Brown, sensed a new assertiveness when some North Island Maori elected a senior chief as a monarch to symbolise Maori unity and be 'joined . . . in accord with the Queen of England; God to be over both'. A minor dispute in the following year gave the governor an opportunity to exercise his authority: one Maori chief, Teira, attempted to sell a piece of land – 600 acres from a total of 1,700,000 in the area – but another, Wiremu King, forbade the sale. Teira's people owned the land, but Wiremu insisted that enough Maori land had been alienated: '. . . their bellies are full with the sight of the money you have promised them'. When Wiremu took the not-very-drastic action of sending some old women to impede the surveyors, Colonel Gore Brown declared martial law and the next Maori War broke out. The fighting, which spluttered on and off for the next decade, cost some two thousand lives and several million pounds, as British troops were sent to reinforce the local militia. As wars went, it was no more than a side-show, but it sparked off an impressive conflict of arguments, pamphlets, parliamentary debates and books, as the relative rights of settlers, Maori and the British taxpayer were disputed.

British governments regarded the Treaty of Waitangi as binding; if the colonists could not manage their own affairs and co-exist peacefully with the Maori, London was not obliged to support them; they were at liberty to try their fortunes elsewhere. Grey was recalled to New Zealand in 1861 and spent the next seven years fighting the Maori, incompetent army officers – he had to take command himself at one point – and the Colonial Office, who were now confirmed in their conviction that colonies were an unnecessary expense. Once again, the fighting ended without a decisive result; on points, the Maori probably won, since the movement begun by Wiremu King quietly continued, and the Maori continued to elect their own monarchs while accepting the colonial constitutional order.

In August 2006 the then current Maori monarch, Dame Arikiavi Te Atairangikaahu, died. She was a descendant of the first king, Te Wherowhero, elected in 1858.

Tawhiao, the second Maori King

From Waitangi we drove south, passing through rolling pastoral hills, dotted with cattle farms, and dramatic cliffs with stunning views to the Pacific, dense forest with palms growing incongruously next to firs until we reached the coastal plain.

Waipu is an unremarkable town with a remarkable history. During the Highland clearances that began after the Scottish were defeated by the English at Culloden in 1746, Highland landlords forcibly disbanded the clan system to make way for sheep farming. In 1817, many such dispossessed Scots journeyed to Canada in search of a new life. In 1850, driven out of Nova Scotia by famine and the inhospitable winters, the Reverend Norman MacLeod organised a mass exodus. Six ships eventually set sail from Canada in 1851, their first landing the south Australian town of Adelaide. There, in the broiling heat, they fared no better then they had in Nova Scotia.

Australia was expensive, following the gold rush, so MacLeod wrote to the governor of New Zealand, asking for land, and in 1853, they landed at Waipu. The Highlanders had the skills necessary to tame the virgin bush and forest so they established a permanent settlement.

The timbered Presbyterian church and a granite monument to the early settlers, crowned with a Scottish lion rampant, recall those pioneering days. On New Year's Day the town hosts a Highland Games at which traditional sports, such as tossing the caber, are played. As we arrived, the sun burst out from behind inky black clouds to light the atmospheric graveyard in which we found ranks of tall white marble head-stones carved with names that were almost all Scottish.

We were soon on our way again, this time to Auckland, the capital of New Zealand until 1865 when it lost its status to Wellington. Since the 1860s' gold rush, when men and women had flooded through the city to the north in search of untold wealth, Auckland has prospered. It remains the largest city in the country, with a population of 1.3 million, and is within easy reach of beaches and countryside. Those who live there claim to enjoy the best lifestyle in the world. With three harbours, almost fifty extinct volcanoes and numerous offshore islands, Auckland is known as the City of Sails. The city hosted the America's Cup in 1999 and 2002, when the downtown Viaduct Harbour was redeveloped, with lively waterside cafés and restaurants. Most Aucklanders have a passion for sailing, and the harbours are packed with boats, commercial and private, from the small and modest to state-of-the-art yachts; we saw one that had allegedly cost a million dollars a metre, contained three more boats, and had a stripe of real gold glistening along its side.

As we drove over the Harbour Bridge for the first time, we were greeted by the lights of downtown Auckland on the southern shore of the Waitemata Harbour, which is dominated by the Sky Tower that rises from the twenty-four-hour Sky City Casino. The gleaming skyscrapers of the financial district contrast with low-rise residential areas, where white-painted colonial weatherboard houses are surrounded by gardens. The city centre is composed of wide, hilly streets filled with shops, but a core of Victorian buildings remains on the road that leads from the university to the sea-front, where the industrial harbour sits next to the new bars and cafés.

By European standards, this felt like a quiet city that got on with things at a steady pace. Even the worst traffic jams didn't seem too bad. The suburbs felt North American, the poorer ones resembling run-down towns in the Midwest. In the glamorous waterside areas, modern whitewashed buildings sat on cliffs with views towards the water and the city centre. Picturesque, green volcanoes emerged at random across the city, giving it its own character and pointing to the uniqueness of Auckland's location; however Western the city might seem, they were a constant reminder that we were still in the Pacific.

In Auckland the sea is everywhere. The bay winds its way in and out of the city confusing your sense of direction: at one moment the water is on the left and the next it's on the right. The nearby island of Rangitoto, which resulted from the most recent volcanic eruption in the region, about six hundred years ago, fills the immediate horizon with the other Hauraki Gulf islands – all sixty-five of them – behind. Some are protected conservation areas while others are holiday resorts, just a ferry ride from the city.

We were keen to find out more about another wave of immigration from the UK: the war brides. The First and Second World Wars prompted migration from Britain to New Zealand, thanks to government-assisted passage schemes. Many New Zealand and Australian servicemen had been stationed in the UK where they met and married their wives. After the war, free passage home was provided for all, but some wives had to sail to New Zealand alone to link up with their husbands.

Leicester Martin was a Mosquito pilot who flew more than sixty missions over Germany during the Second

World War. We met him and his wife, Sylvia, at the Cotton Club in the centre of Auckland next to a busy park graced with a statue of Queen Victoria. The exterior of the building was covered with dead ivy, like something out of the Addams Family.

Leicester was wearing his medals on his dark blue blazer with his regimental tie. We sat in a bar that resembled a London pub, walls hung with sailing pictures and a decoratively plastered high ceiling. Sunk in leather sofas, we were served tea, with dainty cakes and sandwiches.

The couple had met and married in England, then Sylvia had come to New Zealand where she lived with her in-laws until Leicester returned from a posting in America. She remembered that her new mother-in-law had never grown accustomed to the idea of her son having married a British girl. As many as three thousand had wed New Zealanders during the war, but many of the marriages didn't last. When Sylvia arrived in New Zealand, it seemed twenty-five years behind Britain. 'All the houses were painted cream with orange or red roofs. All the factories were built of corrugated iron. Everything was so temporary. The society was very old-fashioned too. The in-laws thought they were being invaded by foreigners who didn't know their ways so they weren't pleased about having us. They were very narrow-minded people.'

What had relationships between Maoris and Europeans been like in those days? 'My great-grandfather came to New Zealand in 1860,' Leicester chipped in. 'The Maori were then quite warlike and a race apart. Some people considered them lazy, so my father, who was in business in Rangiora, would never hire a Maori person. However, as years have gone by, perceptions have changed. When I was a child, we whites kept ourselves to ourselves but now we mix without thinking.'

Sylvia echoed her husband's view: 'Living in middle England, I had never seen a black person until the American troops came over. When I came here, there were very few Maori in the South Island but over the years we have learnt to live with them next door and are friends. We're very multicultural here now, a much more open-minded society than when I first arrived.'

∼ *Maori in Politics* ∼

Here is Petatone
This is the 10 December
The sun shines, and the birds sing . . .
But where is the money?
Three years has this matter in various debates been
*   discussed . . .*
But where is the money?

Maori women sang this verse to welcome Dr Isaac Featherston – Petatone – and Charles Dilke when they arrived in 1866 for a meeting. Featherston was provincial superintendent of the Wellington district, and Dilke, who was radical, republican, but later a Liberal cabinet minister, was one of the first British politicians to visit the colonies ,between 1866 and 1867. The meeting had been arranged to settle the division of the purchase price of some communal-ly owned land, exactly as provided by the Treaty of Waitangi. Since two of the clans claiming the land, the Ngati Apa and the Ngati Raukawa, were recent enemies, it was a tense encounter, which lasted for six days. Every leader spoke, consulted his people, argued with Featherston and with the other clan leaders until they reached agreement. Then the money, £25,000 in gold, was brought from Wellington. On the sixth day the whole population gathered to celebrate with a *haka*.

The problem of Maori participation in the new 'responsible' government was solved by creating four parliamentary seats, the incumbents to be elected by all adult Maori men; it was to be another twelve years before British men were granted the same privilege. The Maori were still under-represented, but they could make themselves felt in political life. By the 1890s a Maori, James Seddon, was a Liberal cabinet minister; it was to be another seventy years before an Australian Aborigine achieved the same distinction.

The relationship between Maori and non-indigenous New Zealanders has been tested throughout their joint history. At Radio Live we sat in on a phone-in hosted by Willie Jackson, a Maori who has been an MP and is now one of New Zealand's foremost political commentators, hosting TV and radio shows. His studio guest was Lindsay Perigo, a right-wing journalist who was once a news presenter on the national station but now speaks out on many national issues.

Lindsay felt the British and other settlers had done the Maori a big favour by settling in New Zealand: 'We saved you from yourselves. We got you to pay attention to the business of living and enjoying life and respecting developing concepts like private property, individual rights, the rule of law, one law for all. The fact that Maori have seven or eight special seats in Parliament says you're incapable of earning parliamentary representation on merit so we have to set aside those seats for you. They have a separate Maori roll that people vote on for these separate Maori MPs. But we have more Maori MPs not representing those seats than representing them. Something like twenty Maori MPs, but still Willie Jackson says, "No, we can't get into Parliament on merit." '

'No,' snapped Willie. 'They set up the Maori seats because they didn't want the Maori in the general seats. They gave us four seats in 1867 when they should have given us sixteen to twenty because there were so many Maori. It's disgusting, what happened. They made laws on our behalf and we had no representation. The apartheid in this country happened against us for years and years. The British betrayed us within a few months of signing the Treaty of Waitangi that guaranteed all our land and possessions. In the 1860s we had the land wars when we fought them to our last breath. Then we wanted to engage with the British and be part of their system.' He admitted that relations had improved, albeit in a limited way. 'There was a lot of resentment but I think that Maori and Pakeha started working together through rugby and through world wars when we signed up to fight with the Pakeha soldiers. But when we came back, we didn't even get pensions!'

They went at it hammer and tongs, until they started to take calls from the public. The equally extreme and much more moderate views that the listeners expressed showed that, despite everything, Maori/European affairs are still complicated and emotive, arousing strong feelings on both sides. One Maori caller voiced her view succinctly: 'Over two hundred years ago, this is what happened to the Maori nation. We had wheatfields, we had flour mills, we had our own banks. We were trading. And today we've been reduced to beggars in our own country. We've had our language stripped away from us. We've had our lands taken. For two generations we've had to put up with someone else's policies. We are expected to stand up and say, "It's OK. Let's move on." We talk about peace but there will never peace in our country until there is justice.'

Willie applauded, and agreed that many Maori feel the same, but also pointed out that, 'A lot of our people have moved on and there's a lot of positivity today.' Another caller dismissed the previous speaker as 'a radical from nowhere', and went on: 'There are three-and-a-half million of us that want this country to flourish, have worked six generations to make it work.'

Lindsay maintained his position, emphasising a fundamental philosophical divide between tribalism and individualism.

The debate raged on without reaching any conclusion – how could it? – but finally Willie expressed a wish for the future: 'I want Maori and Pakeha to work together well, as this bloke [Lindsay Perigo] and I do, even though we're philosophically opposed in a number of areas. I want us to work together like this, to debate, to talk.'

'The best way to do that,' replied Lindsay, claiming the last word, 'is to forget that he's brown and I'm white, and just treat each other as individuals. It comes back to the philosophy of individualism. That is the solution and the salvation.'

We left the studio, little wiser than we had been when we'd gone in, except that we had seen for ourselves evidence of the national debate that rages on as it has since the early days of British imperialism.

We drove out of the city and on to narrow, winding roads through wild, hilly countryside. We were on our way to Bethells, a small town near the rugged coastline west of Auckland that is characterised by volcanic cliffs, ironsand beaches and crashing seas.

From Bethells, a track led down sharply through the forest to the home of Te Rangitu Netana, a *Ta Moko* – tattoo – artist. Te Rangitu is a descendant of the Ngapuhi-Ngatiwai-Tearawa tribe and was brought up with strong Maori beliefs. He learnt elements of Maori art from his father and grandfather, then trained in Maori tribal artistry in Auckland. He is perhaps best known for having tattooed a tribal design on Robbie Williams's upper arm.

He invited us in, and led the way up a winding staircase to the second floor where a largely open-plan living space overlooked the countryside to a distant bay. Images of voluptuous cartoon women, action figures and Maori illustrations hung on the walls. First, he explained the significance of tattooing in Maori culture: 'Traditionally tattoos serve many spiritual and practical functions. Practically, they show where a person was from, their tribal area, what work they did, whether they'd been to war, their medical history, their lineage – their tribal and family history. It's a big thing to know who you are and where you've come from in our culture. It gives you a sense of pride so that you respect yourself and one another.'

In keeping with tradition, Te Rangitu is tattooed all over. 'My tattoos symbolise who I am and represent my dedication to my culture,' he explained, as he showed us, first, those based on his mother's, grandmother's and father's origins. Some patterns represented 'plentiful food and plentiful knowledge' while others were 'spirit patterns'. 'My first tattoo symbolises a wood-pigeon. My father told me that it flies forward in life. You can always hear a wood-pigeon before you see him – that is definitely me!' Anything significant that happens to him is translated into a tattoo on his body.

While he talked to us, he was decorating Janine McGrath, a youth worker from within the Maori community, who told us: 'Tattooing for me is about my identity, about who I am and where I've been. When I started getting tattoos there wasn't *Ta Moko* and all we could access was from sailors or convicts, and that's how we were viewed when we showed our tattoos.' Since the 1980s there has been a resurgence in traditional tattooing and the designs are worn with pride. Te Rangitu explained how the tattoo he was creating on Janine's arm represented her job, looking after young people at risk, counselling them and helping them find a voice in society.

Te Rangitu and Janine gave us insight into Maori pride in their heritage. As far as Te Rangitu is concerned, tattooing is a positive, visual way of restoring one's sense of self worth and helps him identify with his people. 'I see the magic in empowering our people and others so they understand who we are as a people in this world. You hear racist groups saying they must keep their culture and not mix it with others. But, you know, the beautiful thing is that we are all on this earth for some reason and we all bring something to the basket. We all have something to learn and something to teach. I love being able to give something back in this way.'

∼ A Dying Race? ∼

By 1877 the Maori Wars were over, the leaders pardoned. One of the most successful, Riwha Titokowaru, was in business as a seed and grain merchant. Sir George Grey was back in charge, this time as prime minister. He was too autocratic and impatient to be successful in democratic politics, but his government established a national system of free and compulsory primary education, which offered Maoris a choice between mainstream and community schooling, with all instruction – at Maori request – in English. But Grey, in common with most British, saw the Maori as a 'dying race': his government's duty was 'to smooth the pillow'. Fewer than fifty thousand were left, with little resistance to European diseases, while immigration had brought settler numbers to almost half a million.

The future for both races was problematic: New Zealand's natural resources of gold and timber were rapidly being exhausted; the wool industry was faced with Australian competition; poverty was rife, and the government was heavily indebted. All these difficulties vanished, and New Zealand's future prosperity was guaranteed in February 1882 when the barque *Dunedin* sailed for London with a cargo of frozen mutton; three months later the meat was unloaded in perfect condition. That year the first dairy factory opened for business, to provide another item for export in butter. Assured of a steady market in Britain, New Zealand lamb and Anchor butter underpinned the early development of a welfare state for both Maori and settlers.

Sadly we had no time to visit the South Island so we missed the dramatic *Lord of the Rings* scenery, contenting ourselves with beautiful but familiar landscapes reminiscent of the English Peaks or the Cotswolds. Quite simply, it felt like home, which made it quite easy to understand why people would move there. We left with the over-riding impression that the colonising process in New Zealand had been a much more considered and, almost, considerate process than it had been elsewhere. Although there have been misunderstandings between Maori and Pakeha, a status quo has been achieved that is, at least, accepted by the Maoris we met.

James Belich had explained to us how he saw New Zealand today: 'New Zealand has been decolonising from Britain since Britain joined the European Community. Until about 1960, New Zealanders saw themselves as both British and New Zealander, but since the 1970s things have become more complicated and, in a way, more exciting. We've got new inflows of people from Asia and the Pacific. We've also the Maori asserting their identity to a greater extent than before. That is backed by one remarkable fact that doesn't get enough attention. In 1900 less than five per cent of the population was Maori and they all lived in the country. In 2000, fifteen per cent of the population was Maori and they live in the cities.

So, Maori issues can no longer be swept under the carpet by the European majority. Maori are back centre stage where they used to be in the 1860s, and New Zealand Europeans have to come to terms with a future in which they can no longer see themselves totally as British. It's an interesting time because we're groping for a mature cultural identity of our own. I do think that you're beginning to see a more self-confident New Zealander emerge who's not necessarily British or Maori.'

8

Australia

We had a new camera assistant on our crew in New Zealand and Australia. He was from New Zealand, Alex, and we all loved him. He was a brilliant blusher, and if you said a lady word like "breasts" or even "hair straighteners" he would go bright pink, then pull his hood up over his head and down over his face. Well, breasts were never off the menu once we knew that – we mentioned them non-stop. His hood was up and down like a – well, a working girl's underthings, shall we say?

I'd have to look in my diary to be sure, but I think we went from Auckland to the Bay of Islands to Auckland to Sydney and up to Alice Springs. I was charmed to find out that Alice Springs, was named after Alice, the wife of Charles Todd, an impoverished young scientist from Greenwich, who set off for the small colony of South Australia to take up his post as Government Astronomer and Superintendent of Telegraphs. He had a seemingly impossible mission: to string a telegraph wire across one of the last uncrossed colonial wildernesses, and connect Australia with the Home Country.

I had a fascinating book about this, *The Singing Line*, written by the original Alice's great-great-granddaughter, Alice Thomson, and as I stood on the red earth of Alice Springs, I did a huge double-take, and realised I'd met Alice Thomson, that we had the same yoga teacher, and that I could have talked to her before I'd left, if I wasn't so thick and had made the connection earlier. Rats.

Driving to Port Arthur, the penal colony, I spotted a roadside sign for a Tasmanian Devil sanctuary. We couldn't stop as we were hot-footing it to the prison to hear about prisoners so desperate to escape they dressed up in kangaroo skins and tried to hop past the guards.

But on the way back, as the light was fading, we went to see the Tasmanian Devils, and we all stood round an enclosure with our cameras, trying to snap them before it got too dark. They are not, as anyone brought up on cartoons might think, perpetually spinning round on their hind legs and snarling, but they do have massive jaws and very pointy teeth and they make a strange screeching noise. This noise and their black colour led to them being called devils. They're protected now, but their numbers have dropped as they're prone to develop facial cancers. We watched them for ages, as they cavorted about, scrapping with each other and making scary faces. It was too dark to film, and for once we weren't in a mad rush.

Happily, we got into the van. Less happily, we got out again. It had a flat battery. Isabel went into survival mode and started hiding packets of crisps under her seat. It reminded me of the tale I'd just been recounting at Port Arthur – about the escaped convicts who ate each other. They didn't jump straight into cannibalism, they started with something simple, like bread, worked up to a kangaroo-skin jacket, then felt able to tackle something more challenging, like an arm. I looked around the crew, to see if they were wearing anything appetising. No, didn't fancy any of their outerwear. If I got desperate, I'd just have to eat Isabel.

∽ Introduction ∽

Although the existence of Australia had long been known to Europeans, it was not until 1788 that the first settlement was attempted. During Queen Victoria's lifetime the experimental prison colony on the eastern coast expanded into a united country with a population of nearly four million. Its prosperity, founded on gold, fine wool and, later, extensive mineral deposits, made it then the world's richest society and its most advanced democracy. However, Aboriginal rights were disregarded.

At first almost entirely British, with a strict whites-only immigration policy, Australia played a prominent part in both World Wars and is today a leading South East Asian power with a varied population. She still has a monarchy, and is one of the world's most advanced large countries.

One of our first stops down under was an island that had held considerable significance for criminals shipped to Australia. Tasmania is just off the south-eastern coast and its capital, Hobart, is Australia's second oldest city. It is a harbour town that seems to roll off the mountain behind it towards the ocean, and retains some Victorian architecture, although warehouses have been converted into fish restaurants and flats.

The focus of our visit was not the city but Port Arthur, a promontory approximately two hours' drive south, which was established in 1830 as a timber station and a prison settlement for repeat offenders. The prisoners were told there were sharks in the surrounding seas and fierce dogs guarding the narrow spit of land that joined Port Arthur to the mainland, so there was no escape.

Now a site of historic interest, Port Arthur has more than sixty buildings, some restored, like the prison chapel and the commandant's house, while others are left in ruins, such as the church, which was gutted by fire, or the vast penitentiary that once held five hundred inmates. The prison was operative until 1877, having earned a reputation as one of the harshest of its kind, but is now Tasmania's number-one tourist attraction. Surrounded by lawns and trees, it's hard to imagine that somewhere so beautiful has such a brutal past. Two wooded hills descend to the prison where a brook, crossed by several small bridges, flows across the plain.

Inside the prison building, a walkway led round one of the upper storeys. It was here that we met Julia Clark, the interpretations manager. She showed us the windowless cells, which measured about nine feet by four – just wide enough for a hammock, a shelf, a stool and a bucket. The wooden door had a little hatch through which the warders would shove food. From last thing at night until six in the morning, the prisoners were kept in chains. In the morning they were let out into the muster yard to be lined up and counted before prayers.

We stood with Julia in the yard, contemplating the grim existence of the many men who were incarcerated here as she explained what had happened to them: 'The men who came here had been transported to New South Wales, or Van Diemen's Land, then reoffended and were sent here. When they arrived, they were marched off the ship and read about an hour and a half's worth of regulations, all of which they were expected to remember on pain of punishment. Then they were marched either to the prisoners' barracks or to here where they'd be given clothes, then banged up in a cell or dormitory. In the morning and evening they had skilly – baked flour mixed with water and bread – while for their midday meal there was a big cauldron of gristly, fatty salt meat boiled with turnips and potatoes.'

Life for those offenders was tough. 'They would all be heavily chained and either worked in the forests, felling enormous trees and carrying them out, or were sent to quarry stone for the Port Arthur buildings or, later, if they were exceptionally bad, they'd be sent to the worst place of all – the coal mines. A lot of men came here for anything between seven and twenty-one years. If they kept reoffending, time was simply added to their sentence so they might be here for as long as forty years. Many went to Hobart, reverted to their criminal ways and found themselves back here. You see the same names going round and round the system. Many ended up in the lunatic asylum or the paupers' depots, shattered by what had been done to them and completely institutionalised. A few were lucky enough to get married, and they seemed to be the ones who stayed out of trouble.'

In the mid-nineteenth century, it became apparent that beating men or physically intimidating them wasn't enough to break them, and solitary confinement was introduced. For twenty-three hours a day, they were locked in their cells, with one hour's exercise, shuffling up and down a small brick yard. 'The big treat was chapel three times a week, when they could sing. But solitary confinement drove people mad rather than reforming them.'

Skilled men sometimes avoided the mines: they were sent to work in the dockyards or perhaps the boot-making shop. Those who didn't reoffend were taught a trade. 'There was no doubt that the men were here to be punished severely but Governor Arthur was keen on rehabilitation and reform. He felt that the opportunity to learn a trade or to read and write gave them an incentive to behave well. Some even ended up as quite distinguished citizens. An ex-convict, not one who had come through Port Arthur, founded the *Mercury* newspaper and another became a distinguished member of the Royal Society.'

Perhaps the most shocking stories were about transported children, aged mainly between twelve and seventeen. 'The youngest was nine,' Julia told us. 'Young James Lynch was transported for stealing three boxes of toys. As far as I know he served his time and got out. Others came from the slums of England's industrial cities. Many of them had been abandoned. Walter Paisley was constantly in trouble and spent a lot of time in solitary but learnt to build boats. One of his can be seen in the Maritime Museum in Hobart.'

∼ An Agreeable Spot ∼

For nearly two centuries after the first European sailors bumped – literally – into Australia no one bothered to explore it. As a matter of form, Captain Cook claimed it for King George III when he landed in 1770, but no one was interested. In 1786 when the British government was debating where to send convicts, now that the former American colonies had refused to accept them, someone suggested Australia. Africa had been considered and rejected, as the climate was fatally unhealthy – perhaps not a bad thing, some thought. Then Sir Joseph Banks, who had sailed with Cook, mentioned an agreeable spot named Botany Bay, which had the added advantage of being far from home: convicts would be unlikely to return. Also, they might, perhaps, 'remain honest, for Want of a Temptation to be otherwise'.

In January 1788 the First Fleet arrived in Australia, an ill-chosen date: in the following year the French Revolution broke out, followed by the Napoleonic Wars, and the little convict settlement was all but forgotten for twenty-five years. In 1819, the year of Queen Victoria's birth, a commissioner was sent to investigate. He found a white population of 30,296; the number of Aborigines was unknown, but must have been in the hundreds of thousands. New South Wales, the first colony, was still little more than a prison settlement: Sydney's Hyde Park convict barracks, still standing in Macquarie Street, was opened that year, to accommodate six hundred male prisoners, and its architect, Francis Greenway, drew up plans for the Female Factory, to house three hundred women.

By 1837, the year of Victoria's accession to the throne, the Australian white population had risen to 132,000. Many were time-served or pardoned convicts and a great majority 'Persons in Humble Life', for whom Eliza Darling, the governor's wife, published *Simple Rules for Guidance*. Two new colonies had been created: Van Diemen's Land (Tasmania), with a large convict population, and South Australia, which was evangelical and convict-free. A third was forming around the small community recently established at the head of Port Philip Bay, variously known as Batmania, after the first settler, John Batman, Glenelg, (after the then Colonial Secretary), or Beargrass. When Governor Sir Richard Bourke visited the town, having made the twelve-day journey from Sydney, he named it after the Queen's 'dear, kind Lord Melbourne', her first Prime Minister.

Captain Cooke takes formal possession of New South Wales in 1770: Joseph Banks is to his right

On 11 November 1850, a coach galloped into Melbourne with a publican sounding a trumpet, waving a Union flag, and shouting, 'Hooray! We've got separation at last!' The news had just arrived that Port Philip, previously part of

New South Wales, was to become the fourth Australian colony, to be known as Victoria, seventeen years after the first settlers had crossed the Bass Strait from Tasmania.

For fifty years after its first settlement, in 1804, Tasmania remained the most violent of the Australian colonies. Bushrangers – escaped convicts – and colonists murdered hundreds of Aborigines who, of course, retaliated. In 1830, Governor George Arthur attempted to round up the survivors. Some were persuaded to settle, and their descendants today represent the island's original population.

Australian governments found Tasmanian institutions convenient for punishing reoffending convicts. Macquarie Harbour prison gained such a vile reputation that a modern gaol was built at Port Arthur. It proved a formidable deterrent: only 10 per cent of the time-served convicts were sent back.

Life in Australia clings to the coast. Out of the plane window, as we flew from Tasmania towards the Northern Territory, the dry red dust of the Australian outback stretched as far as the eye could see. Known as the Red Centre, the land is largely flat, except for the McDonnell mountain ranges that run from north to south both east and west of Alice Springs.

For thousands of years, only the nomadic Aranda Aborigines moved through this inhospitable landscape, stopping at water-holes. The one at Alice Springs made an obvious staging-post so a small white settlement was established there. Today it is a modern city with a population that has grown from twelve people in 1899 to almost thirty thousand. Tourists use it as a base to explore the surrounding area. Because everything has to be brought into the town from miles away, prices are uniformly high. Our taxi driver took us to the top of Anzac Hill, which offers a fine view of the city and of the mountain range in the distance. Low-lying white houses bleached by the sun flank wide roads.

The centre of town is a compact grid that contains most of the city's hotels and restaurants; Todd Street Mall is a lively pedestrian precinct with shopping arcades and a Sunday market. The oldest surviving building is the modest brick Stuart Town Gaol, a building that was used from 1909 to 1938, and not far away Adelaide House, originally a hospital but now a museum, was opened in 1926.

∽ *Terra Nullius* ∽

The first European reports of '*Terra Australis*' were not encouraging: '. . . the most arid and barren region . . . the inhabitants, too, are the most wretched and poorest creatures', and there appeared to be few of them. When Captain Cook landed there, Australia was '*terra nullius*', a region without organised government.

It was another two centuries before Aboriginal rights were formally acknowledged. In part this was due to their fragmentation; there were perhaps half a million scattered over the continent, sharing common traditions, but forming no unit larger than a clan. New Zealand Maori chiefs, providing they observed traditional custom, could deliver firm agreements and deploy enough force to compel colonial

John Batman negotiates with Aborigines

administrations to pay attention to their grievances. Australian Aboriginal communities were too small to make this easy, and colonial administrations lacked the will to try.

British reformers saw dispossessed Aborigines as no better off than slaves and attempted to protect them: in South Australia it was made a condition that 'no lands in occupation or enjoyment be offered for sale unless previously ceded by the Natives . . .'. It was one thing for British governments to legislate but another to ensure that the conditions laid down were observed. Many bloody battles, often unrecorded, were fought between the settlers and the Aborigines. Before colonies became self-governing, those accused of killing Aborigines were tried and – at least on one famous occasion after the Myall Creek massacre – executed; after imperial control had been removed, trials became rarer. An attempt was made to integrate Aborigines into colonial society with the establishment of a mounted Aboriginal police force after the style of the Cape Mounted Rifles, the famous Khoikhoi regiment in South Africa, but the corps was disbanded as soon as an independent colonial administration was elected.

We had come to Alice Springs to see 'outback' Australia and to meet some of its indigenous people. Arthur Achee is, apparently, the oldest and most authoritative Aborigine in the area, so we were invited to meet him and his grandson Tommy – who played the didgeridoo for us, a stirring, primeval sound. He also made a painting to give us an idea of aboriginal culture. He used the deep red and ochre of the landscape in patterns of dots to depict the geckos and kangaroos we saw around us.

Arthur took us out of town near to the Telegraph Station where the original settlement buildings still stand. The Station was established in 1872 to relay messages between Darwin and Adelaide. It remains the best preserved of the stations on the Overland Telegraph line. We walked across a dry river-bed and along one of the paths that snake around this part of the outback to sit on a rocky outcrop close to several eucalyptus trees. Once, these paths had been the only routes from the Telegraph Station to the town, but now locals use them on an evening stroll. As the rocks turned from orange to deep red in the setting sun, and rock wallabies hopped around

AUSTRALIA

Hobart, Tasmania. Mount Wellington towers above this very British city on the edge of the world.

This is one of those photographic studios where you can dress up as a Victorian Lady. I didn't go in.

The exercise yard and crumbling penitentiary building at the infamous Port Arthur Penal Colony.

Tommy Achee, one of the last of the Simpson clan, plays a traditional, haunting rhythm.

Arthur Achee, who told us about aboriginal traditions and the experience of his people since coming into contact with Europeans.

Les Hiddins has a tucker bag full of vile-tasting bugs. I did eat one. Well, half of one. Well, a bit of one . . .

Tommy Achee paints in a traditional Aboriginal style, using dots of paint to depict a lizard.

Wendy Huggins in her role as Ned Kelly's mother, at Old Melbourne Gaol. All together – 'On Mother Kelly's doorstep . . .'

Margaret Humphrie of the Child Migrant Trust with Harold Haig, who was wrongly told he was an orphan and brought to Australia aged ten.

This is the pier where the child migrants got their first sight of Australia, after six weeks at sea.

Robyn Annear, a Ballarat historian and author of *Nothing But Gold* – a brilliant account of the Australian Gold Rush.

Once I got over my disappointment that Tasmanian Devils are not as cute as Taz in the cartoon, I was thrilled to see them in real life.

ZAMBIA

Under the same tree where David Livingstone met the Toka Leya people, I chatted with the chieftainess, Bedyango.

The children show great interest in us filming in Mukuni village.

Taking advice from Amos, a traditional Zambian herbalist in Livingstone market.

Natural Viagra for sale at Livingstone Market.

Some of the first white settlers in Northern Rhodesia, now Zambia, are buried here at Old Drift, now a game reserve.

Victoria Falls.
In full flow, the water
cascades along the
entire width, but even
in the dry season it is a
stunning sight.

Sunset on the Zambezi river – that ripple
is a hippo popping up.

us, we asked Arthur how the Aborigines had lived before the arrival of Europeans.

'They lived the same for thousands and thousands of years,' he replied. 'Westerners constantly evolved from the Stone Age to the Bronze Age to the Iron Age, finding new technologies for doing things. The Aborigines weren't like that. They had one way of living. They were nomadic in the sense that they had to know exactly where the food was and where the water was – the two came together. They had to know about the climate and the seasons, and about the food chain that was above and below the ground. They found what Mother Nature had to give. The women went hunting for berries, eggs, seeds and things like that, while the men went for kangaroos and emus. With Aboriginal people it's about sharing and caring, integration and responsibility to one another.'

Equipped with only the basic weapons they needed for survival – spears and boomerangs – the Aborigines were no match for the white men with their guns. 'If we'd had the same type of weaponry we'd have made a fight of it,' said Arthur. Instead they could resort only to guerrilla warfare, which made little difference. 'With the assimilation process, a lot of bad things happened,' Arthur went on. 'Massacres of men, women and children happened across Australia, with more frequency in the coastal areas where most of the first contact took place. It's sad to hear the stories of women running away with their babies and being shot down by men on horseback. People try to cover those realities up but they can't because they're handed down through generations.'

Arthur was insistent that the Aboriginal identity is still important to many, some of whom prefer to live in the bush by the old ways. Many use ancient methods of communication, telling stories through the dot symbols in their paintings. 'Now they are selling them as a form of art to survive.' Originally they had no commerce and no need for money because what they needed was all around them. 'Today we know there's plenty more where the last meal came from. But Aboriginal people didn't. They cherished what they had because they had to make it last for two or three days.' Aborigines were left on the fringes of European settlements or in inhospitable regions, their spiritual and cultural ties with their land broken.

It wasn't until 1967 that a constitutional referendum was passed to include Aborigines in Australia's national census. At the same time, though, came unemployment and access to alcohol. 'Now alcohol, drugs and substance abuse are killing our people. Our kids these days have nothing to do. Everything's been taken away from them and they're looking for leadership, but all the leaders have gone. So they're lost.'

∼ Another Planet? ∼

By 1861 Melbourne's population had risen to more than 140,000, higher than those of Bristol and Sydney, and it had become the undisputed centre of Australian finance. New South Wales, Victoria, South Australia, Tasmania and Queensland all had responsible governments that enabled them to act in most matters as independent nations. Victoria, New South Wales and South Australia had their own navies and militia and began to assert themselves abroad. When France threatened to annex the New Hebrides, Victoria put its navy on a war footing, and when Germany threatened New Guinea, the Queensland premier, Thomas McIlwraith, simply took over the eastern half of the island. Colonial secretary Lord Derby was astounded: did the colonists 'want another planet all to themselves? They seemed to think it would be a desirable arrangement, if only it were feasible. The magnitude of their ideas is appalling . . . it is certainly hard for four million of English settlers to have only a country as big as Europe to fill up.'

The actual size of Australia was only now being discovered. In 1819 only the region around Sydney and the island of Tasmania had been mapped. By 1842 Edward Eyre had crossed the continent from east to west, finding little but scrub and sand. In August 1860 the Victorian Exploration Expedition, led by Robert O'Hara Burke and William James Wills, left from Melbourne with twenty-six camels, twenty-three horses and six wagons. Only the two leaders succeeded in reaching the Gulf of Carpentaria, on foot, and both perished on the way back. A few years later, John Mc Dougall Stuart left from Adelaide with a smaller party. He completed the journey and came back alive.

The death of Robert Burke

When Les Hiddins was in the Australian Army he did two tours of duty in Vietnam, and became the main author of the *Army Combat Guide* (1987). After his retirement, in 1989, he continued in the army reserves and became Australian ABC TV's *Bush Tucker Man*; he is an expert in survival and native bush food, well placed to tell us about the European exploration of the outback and, specifically, the doomed expedition of Burke and Wills.

'Well, it was a cock-up from start to finish. Other south-Australian states were exploring but Victoria had done nothing so the Royal Society in Melbourne decided to put together an expedition to cross the continent and back. There was some colonial kudos to be had in being the first expedition to succeed. In 1860, Robert O'Hara Burke was announced as the leader, with George James Landells as his number two and William James Wills as his number three. Why Burke got the job I'm unsure, because he knew nothing about the bush and took far more equipment than they needed. The entourage was like a circus with sixteen men, horses, camels and so much gear. They even carried gallons of rum for the camels, and folding boats in case they found an inland sea.' They had this quaint idea of spreading Englishness to the natives as they travelled so they gave Union Jack handkerchiefs to the local Aborigines. By the time they got round the Murray river, they were getting messages from Melbourne saying that they were spending too much money so they laid people off and auctioned some of the gear.

'They eventually got as far as Cooper's Creek where they put their final depot. By this time there was only a small group – they had left the others in staging depots along the way. Burke led a mad dash to get to the Gulf of Carpentaria with Wills, Gray and King. On the return leg, Gray died, so the other three spent a day digging a grave and burying him. That day cost them dear because, when they returned to Cooper's Creek, they found the rest of their party had left that morning, having carved a message on a tree, now known as the Dig Tree, that told them where some rations were buried. The three men tried to walk towards Adelaide but after about a week, they returned to the Dig Tree where Burke and Wills died.'

Might they have had a chance of survival if Burke and Wills had handled things differently? 'On the way north, their attitude to the Aborigines wasn't real bright. They looked down their noses at them and didn't roll with the countryside one little bit. But when they got hungry, they took notice of what the Aborigines were eating. What eventually killed them was the cakes they made out of the seeds of the nardoo plant. They didn't know how to prepare them properly so they were slowly poisoned. If they'd familiarised themselves with bush tucker earlier in their journey they might have survived.'

Les showed us what he meant. First he broke a blood-wood apple from a eucalypt. 'Right inside there's a little insect, which is edible.' He dug it out and offered it to us. It tasted like bitter coconut. Next on the menu was bush banana, an oval green fruit that grows on a vine. Inside, seeds resembling those of a cucumber or melon tasted like peas. However, to survive in the bush water, of course, is essential. 'Watch the parrots and other bird life. They're all grain eaters and at the end of the day they go straight to water. They will lead you to a local water source. You can find little rock holes, or look where one set of animal tracks joins another – they're always pointing towards water.'

∾ *Pentonvillains* ∾

The idea of Australia as a series of penal settlements needs some modification. New South Wales and Van Diemen's Land were certainly intended as such, and theoretically, as it is part of New South Wales, Port Philip should have been obliged to accept convicts. In practice, none were ever landed there. The fifteen hundred who came against their will between 1844 and 1848 were 'Exiles', or Pentonvillains, conditionally pardoned having served a short sentence and free to bring with them their wives and families. This was too much for the locals: the last shipment of exiles was turned away, and sent to Sydney. Victoria's population was, therefore, composed largely of energetic and industrious – usually literate and opinionated – settlers, with no worries about the 'convict stain'.

A strikingly European city in flavour, Melbourne's central landscaped gardens and parks look English, and in the central business district, the elaborate nineteenth-century façades recall the city's Victorian heyday. Of all the Australian cities, Melbourne has the most elaborate period architecture, from the town hall, built with gold-rush profits, and the gothic St Paul's Cathedral to Flinders Street station and the State Library. Widely thought of as

Australia's cultural centre, Melbourne has a lively arts scene, which includes a huge new complex by the river, and streets of glamorous shops.

Our first stop was at the Old Melbourne Gaol where, for years, lunatics and hardened criminals were kept under lock and key. We arrived at sunset, and walked through the main gates into the central courtyard, then entered the eerie bluestone prison. Even though much of the building has been demolished, the atmosphere is still chilling. The prisoners who languished here were subject to solitary confinement, chained, flogged and sometimes executed; a hundred and thirty-five hangings were carried out between 1845 and 1929. The most famous was that of Ned Kelly on 11 November 1880; near the entrance, his death mask stares out of a glass case, with his armour displayed on either side and his gun on a plinth in front of it. Many more death masks, made in the interests of phrenology, are displayed throughout the building. The prison has several floors, with long corridors of tiny cells.

Suddenly, a wild-haired figure in a long black cloak and gloves, was rushing towards us. We froze – then recognised Wendy Huggins, an actress, who was dressed as Ned Kelly's mother. She had come to tell us his story.

∼ Irish Troubles ∼

Queen Victoria took a personal interest in the colony that had been named after her. When the search was on for a new Governor in 1854 – a sensitive appointment only eighteen months after the violent protest of the miners at the Eureka hotel in Ballarat (see page 243) – she opposed the selection of James Wilson, founding editor of the *Economist*, for 'so large and important a colony'. 'It ought,' the Queen considered, 'to be a man of higher position and standing,' rather than a journalist – and former tradesman. Melbourne reciprocated her regard: two theatres, the Victoria and the Queens Theatre Royal were named after her, along with Queen Victoria Market.

An unfortunate incident damaged Melbourne's reputation in the Queen's eyes. Although Victoria never visited the colonies she encouraged her family to do so, and in 1867–8 her second son Prince Alfred, Duke of Edinburgh, made the first royal visit to Australia. Then twenty-two, Alfred was in command of HMS *Galatea*. It was a sensitive time: the Queen herself had been threatened with an assassination attempt by Irish nationalist 'Fenians', the precursors of the IRA, and the threat was real enough – there were four attempts on her life during her reign, and seventeen Londoners were killed by a Fenian bomb in 1867. Although the Queen, who despised such threats, refused to take any precautions – 'Such a bore', she complained – she was horrified to hear in February 1868 that Prince Alfred had been shot by Melbourne Irishman, Henry O'Farrell. The Prince recovered, but O'Farrell was tried and hanged, in spite of the Prince's appeal for clemency. There had been no plot: O'Farrell was clinically insane.

∼ The True Story of the Kelly Gang ∼

Australia was a land of opportunity, and although the Scots, as the visiting politician Charles Dilke recorded, were as successful there as they were 'everywhere in the known world',

Irish immigrants prospered more easily than did Irish Americans. As a result, according to the Irish Nationalist MP Michael Davitt, Irish Australians were usually 'sharers in the sentiment of Australian attachment to the Empire' and often displayed in their cabins a picture of the Queen, 'almost always flanked by that of Mr Gladstone'.

A disproportionate number of criminals, though, were Irish – twenty-one out of the twenty-seven convicted of armed robbery in New South Wales in 1872 – and one Victorian gang found its way into popular mythology. It is not unusual for murderers to become infamous: several books have been written about the still-unidentified 'Jack the Ripper', and the scene of his crimes has become a tourist attraction, but the elevation of Ned Kelly, a brutal thug, to popular hero, an icon of Australia, needs some explanation. The facts are simple enough: the Kelly boys, Ned and Dan, formed a gang with two other young men, and ambushed a police patrol; a fight followed, in which Ned personally killed two troopers. It was two years before the gang was caught, tracked by Aboriginal police to the little Victorian town of Glenrowan; Ned survived the subsequent firefight to be tried – by an Irish judge – and hanged.

Ned Kelly, a dramatic figure in his home-made armour

His fame is partly due to a self-exculpatory letter he wrote – most criminals attempt to find excuses –

but primarily because of the bizarre armour the gang forged out of plough mould-boards, which inspired Sir Sidney Nolan's famous series of paintings. The true heroes were the Aboriginal police, who ran the gang down, but the myth endures.

From the sombre experience of the gaol, we drove to Station Pier, just fifteen minutes from the centre of town to the north of Port Philip Bay. This is Australia's largest cargo and container port. More than that, the pier was the point of arrival for millions of migrants from 1854 until 1977. Another pier is dedicated to the Tasmania passenger ferry but the area has also been developed into flats. The red and white gatehouse looks as it must have done more than a hundred years ago when thousands of men landed during the gold-rush hoping to make their fortune. The first Australian railway line ran between here (then known as Sandridge) and Melbourne, built in the mid-nineteenth century so travellers no longer had to lug their belongings along tracks running through swamps to the city. Today, there are cafés and restaurants, even one that serves dog food for those who want to pamper their pooch.

The gold-rush was not what had brought us here, but the shocking subject of child migration – which the British and Australian governments have never explained. We met Margaret Humphries, who set up the Child Migrant Trust, and Harold Haig, who had been one of those children sent from Britain to Australia. We sat in a café at the end of the pier looking out at the waves through the big windows and, as we talked, a strong sea breeze battered the cane blinds against the glass roof over our heads.

Margaret was a qualified social worker working in the English adoption service when a woman wrote to her saying she had been in a children's home in England. When she was four, she was told that her parents had died, then put on a boat to Australia with lots of other children. 'I thought that really couldn't be right,' Margaret told us, 'but after meeting her and investigating, I found that it was.'

As a result Margaret went on to research Britain's child-migration policy in the post-Second World War years, and the lives of a hundred and thirty thousand children and their families. She found that many children in British residential care were told that their parents were dead and were asked if they'd like to go to Australia – a land of sweets, sunshine, houses on the beach and horse rides to school – then shipped there without birth certificates, passports or any other documentation. Others were sent to Canada. This was a Commonwealth scheme whereby, in this case, Australia gained numerous white children (black children were excluded) and Britain emptied its children's homes. 'The youngest child was three and the oldest fourteen, but they tended to be between six and twelve.'

'The kids mainly thought Australia was just round the corner or that they would be able to swim home, so having to stay on a boat for six weeks came as a big shock. Others were told they would be met by and live with loving families who desperately wanted them. Of course, there were no such families. There were no death certificates for their parents so it could never be proved that they were orphans and therefore eligible for adoption. As a result they were sent into large institutions.'

This had been Harold's experience. His parents had separated during the war and he was put into care in East Sussex while his sister was sent to the Salvation Army, who arranged for her to be adopted when she was ten. Harold has blocked out almost all his memories of what happened to him when he was shipped to Australia at the age of eleven: 'I was in a boys' home till I was fourteen then I started work and went into the boys' hostel next door where I stayed until I was probably eighteen.' What did he think had been the long-term effects of his uprooting? 'You learn not to trust people and not to let your emotions out. You protect yourself. It was hard to become a father because I didn't know what to do. I had no role model.'

Margaret agreed that all the children suffered in the same way to a greater or lesser degree. 'It's a general experience of lack of love, lack of being helped to feel individual. Harold has said many times in the past that he felt he had a big hole or an iceberg inside him. Life in those institutions was very regimented, and many of the children were physically and sexually abused for years and had no one to turn to.'

Margaret was brought into contact with Harold by his sister, Marie, who had had a strong recollection of a brother and was determined to find him. 'How could you have a situation where one child had permanency and family life in England while her full brother had been sent to the other side of the world? How could that happen?' Margaret asked. 'You can't make sense of it until you have some understanding of Britain's fairly shameful childcare policy. These migrant schemes weren't about the children or their families but about political objectives and economic issues. They robbed children of family life and of their identity.' Many parents were told their children had died. We could only imagine their shock when, fifty or so years later, they heard that they were alive in Australia.

As the years pass, the trust's work in reuniting these families has become a race against time. 'We're now at a point where family members are dying while we're looking for them. We did eighteen reunions last year, which is a lot of work, a lot of planning and very hard for everyone involved. Of course, none of us can give parents their children back or people like Harold their childhood. But we have to do everything we can to give people their background, their identity, their family history and help them make sense of it.'

Harold was reunited with his sister after ten years of searching, but it was too late for them to meet their parents. Their mother had died the year before they met and by the time they traced their father, four years later, he had died too.

Where Margaret's priority is to find families, Harold and his friends are concerned with compensation for the deported children and those who suffered abuse in Australian children's homes. But, as Margaret explained, it is an area fraught with difficulties. 'Trying to get two governments to come to the table and look at a restitution policy for all involved is extraordinarily difficult because we are still in partial denial of what happened to the children who are living with lifelong injustice.

If we allow this to carry on not being resolved, then the responsibility is ours as well.'

Harold is representative of many children. The anger he feels at having been robbed of so much is directed at the British and Australian governments. 'They chose to send us to the other side of the world and forget about us, and Australia had no trouble working with England. But when, many years later, it's brought to their attention, they refuse to deal with it adequately. We need a judicial inquiry to treat the issue seriously and to organise compensation.'

Margaret agrees. 'That's the only way the child migrants as a community will feel that they've received justice and recognition and there may be a point where some recovery can start.'

We were impressed by what Margaret had told us about the Trust's extraordinary work, and appalled by the suffering inflicted on so many with the British government's complicity. First convicts, then children. Had Australia been seen simply as a convenient dumping ground for society's rejects – so far away that we could pretend they didn't exist?

But Australia did have one resource that brought people flooding in of their own accord in the last half of the nineteenth century. Gold.

∼ The Golden Fleece ∼

By 1850 Victoria was already prosperous, thanks to the merino sheep, with its famously fine wool, which produced the lightest and most expensive cloth. It was soon to become richer still.

Driving sheep from a bush fire

In August 1851 a huge gold nugget was discovered at Ballarat, seventy miles north-west of Melbourne, and prospectors poured in from all over the world, including many from the earlier diggings in California. In comparison with the latter it was an orderly goldfield. Robert Cecil, later Lord Salisbury, found 'more civility than I should be likely to find in the good town of Hatfield', even though he was wearing a white top hat. But the population of Victoria doubled rapidly, then trebled, and proved difficult for the new colonial administration to control.

In London, Lord John Russell's Liberal government had already decided that the Australian colonies were to be allowed to design their own constitutions, with whatever qualifications for the vote they chose, appreciating that these might be more democratic than what prevailed in Britain, and that they might also choose soon to become independent. They were free, should they wish, to resign from the Empire. At the time few politicians expected that, a hundred and fifty years later, Victoria's great-great-granddaughter would be Queen of Australia.

Sifting gold from a river bed

∼ *Eureka* ∼

Victorian politicians' attempts to agree a constitution with their electorate were complicated by the thousands of prospectors, who were insisting on being included on the voters' lists alongside the existing settlers. As long as the tactful and humorous governor of Victoria, Charles La Trobe, was in charge a balance was held. He had arrived in Port Philip in 1839 and was universally popular, but his successor Sir Charles Hotham, who took up the post in June 1854, was dictatorial and disliked. Disregarding all advice, he enforced payment of the licence fees due from the diggers and insisted on intolerably frequent inspections. Six months later a banal pub brawl outside the Eureka Hotel in Ballarat led to a violent riot, with the diggers mustering behind a stockade, flying their own flag. The army and police attacked, leaving thirty-four dead.

The fight at the Eureka stockade passed into Australian myth as a great example of the struggle for liberty but, like most myths, this was not quite the truth: the miners' demands had already been conceded by the colonial government. When it was clear that no jury was willing to convict, the trials of the surviving rebels were speedily dismissed, and their leader, the Irishman Peter Lalor, became an elected member of the new colonial administration.

On the way to Ballarat, where gold had been discovered in 1851, we drove through a rolling agricultural landscape to a large town with buildings that reflected the wealth it had accrued from gold. The tents that covered the surrounding areas and the thousands of people who came here hoping to make their fortune are long gone, but for twenty years Ballarat was at the centre of the search for gold.

Originally a small agricultural town built on Lake Wendouree, Ballarat blossomed with its new-found wealth. Many grandiose buildings were designed and constructed in Lydiard Street to accommodate the town's new needs: the railway station, the four banks, Her Majesty's Theatre and Craig's Royal Hotel, one of more than fifty that survive from the gold-rush days. The gold-field was productive for a hundred years, so Ballarat thrived, prospered and expanded, with suburbs that now cover most of the diggings. In other outlying towns, some of them ghost towns now, relics still exist of that time when one of the great mass migrations of the nineteenth century took place.

We arrived in miserable weather so took shelter in our hotel where we met Robyn Annear, a local historian who painted a vivid picture of life in the goldfields: 'A couple of hundred thousand came between the discovery of gold and the end of 1852, so that made a big difference to the place. Anyone with a shovel and a permit could come, except the Chinese who, in 1854, had restrictions clapped on them. They had to pay a substantial landing tax so they simply went to a port across the border in south Australia and trekked overland for a couple of hundred miles to the goldfields. That's how keen they were.'

People left their homes to embark on a hazardous journey across the world on the strength of what might have been a rumour. 'They were incredibly relieved when they arrived at Melbourne,' Robyn said. 'As they made their way north-west towards Ballarat, they heard the gold-fields before they saw them. They heard the sound of picks, then saw thousands of people strung along the creek banks rinsing the gravel in tin dishes. Once you've got the wrist action, in the space of a few minutes you'd be left with a bit of sand and, if you were lucky, a glint of gold. They'd also hear the cradles, wooden boxes that were rocked with a stick that worked the gravel through several layers. They were riotous on the ear, like thousands of cement mixers.'

But there was more to it than just turning up, buying a permit and marking out a claim: 'A lot of men became domesticated. People dug in parties of four or five and one man was the tent-keeper, essentially the "wife" of the party. He stayed behind, did the cooking and bore the wrath of the others if the chops were overdone.'

The only way to find people was by their flags and the decorations on their tents. For some of the men, it was the first time they had experienced such freedom, living with-out anyone to answer to. 'Every man was his own master with his gold dust kept tied up in a knot in his hanky or in a cylindrical matchbox. People paid for everything in gold and prices were hugely inflated. For instance it cost many ounces of gold to buy enough flour each week to make their damper [bread].'

'They would have a camp oven, a big iron pot on feet, which they stuck in the coals. The bread was just flour and water rolled into a round or an oval, stuck into the pot and left with the lid on until it was black. They drank lots of black tea. Any fresh food, apart from off-the-hoof meat, was hard to come by.'

These wild-haired, bearded men 'wore pale moleskins with red and blue flannel shirts, big boots and a big belt. Archaeologists digging in the Victorian goldfields have found fantastic brass belt buckles, often depicting cricket scenes. They had quite a bit of weaponry, too, that they fired every night. Some say it was to let the neighbours know you were armed but it was also to clean the guns. It was like fireworks every night.'

It sounded to us like the camping holiday from hell, albeit with an optimistic spirit. 'There were lots of trees in the valleys leading to the creeks so they had massive campfires every night where they'd sit with their neighbours and chew the fat about how they'd done that day and what they'd do when they struck it rich.'

Plenty of others made money on the back of the men in the fields by supplying accommodation on the way, food and equipment. In 1851 there were even a few women, who tended to make a living from prostitution or 'sly grogging', selling alcohol. But what happened to the men panning for gold? 'A lot of them made fortunes,' Robyn said. 'Some didn't. Some made enough to buy a farm, settle their families and build a future. But it could be a long slog for many people that usually lasted a couple of months.

'Later on women came as part of family groups with kids. My family was on the diggings in 1852: my great-great-grandfather and -mother, their four children and one on the way. Later they wrote about the excitement of it, of trawling around in the diggings after the rain and going over people's spoil heaps – the dirt thrown out of the holes. Kids could get away with that. It was just a great adventure with a bit of school thrown in.'

～ *Colonial Rivalries* ～

The near-four million inhabitants of Australia were beginning to consider that federation might be a sound plan, but rivalries were still keen, especially between the two largest colonies, Victoria and New South Wales – both contenders for leadership. In 1864 a proposal for customs union had already collapsed when armed conflict threatened between the two colonies on the Murray river. South Australia, New South Wales and Victoria, ignoring any common benefits, built their railways to different gauges; a journey between the two largest cities required passengers and freight to change trains half-way. When Sydney built a great exhibition hall, Melbourne's had to be larger, but both were completed with the extraordinary speed and efficiency that characterised nineteenth-century engineering. Should Adelaide or Melbourne be the terminus of the transcontinental railway? Adelaide won, and South Australia's borders were pushed north to the Timor Sea. The colonial capitals

Train trips in Australia could be complicated, with three different gauges of rail track in different states

sneered at each other. One traveller remarked that Sydney folk were 'frightfully rich – but mostly descended from convicts – and as for their behaviour!'. In an ancient Sydney joke, a mother says she has five children: three living and two in Melbourne.

At the outbreak of the Anglo-Boer War, in October 1899, Canada and New Zealand sent national contingents to help the imperial cause; Australian troops came as representatives of their own colonies, with accompanying jealousies. Writing to his old college friend Lord Milner, Basil Wise, the South African High Commissioner of New South Wales, complained that officers from Victoria were being given the best posts, although 'it is certain that the New South Wales troops, both in officers, men and equipment, are superior in a marked degree'. However, in little more than a year, a national Australian army was fighting in South Africa.

Common sense prevailed, if slowly. The debate on federation, which continued in Australia between 1885 and 1900, remains probably the best example of democracy in action. Without war or revolution, in civil and reasonable debate, a new country was constructed. After only forty years of democratic government – but with centuries of British constitutional tradition – Australians designed their future. On 1 January 1901, Queen Victoria was able to congratulate her new dominion: six colonies, self-governing for nearly half a century, were united in the new Commonwealth of Australia, with a population of 3,773,801 (whites; Aborigines were not counted and perhaps numbered 95,000).

∼ *The Second Commonwealth* ∼

As expected, choosing a capital proved difficult. Melbourne and Sydney both claimed the distinction, and the other states grudgingly acquiesced. Honour was eventually satisfied by choosing Canserra in New South Wales at least a hundred miles from Sydney; in the meantime, Parliament could meet in the 1880 Melbourne Exhibition Building, in Carlton Gardens. It had been designed by the father of Melbourne's most famous citizen, Helen Mitchell, better known as Dame Nellie Melba.

Australia was to be, in many respects, the world's most advanced democracy – New Zealand always excepted, with votes for women twenty years before Britain – but the constitution had two flaws. Unless Aborigines already had voting rights in their own states, they were not admitted to the franchise, and the 'White Australia' policy was firmly enforced: all immigrants must be European and preferably British (even Italians were frowned upon). It was a shameful state of affairs that still troubles Australia.

Australia is vast. We left, still trying to absorb everything that we'd seen and heard. The uncomfortable ever-present reality, though, is that when the British arrived there didn't seem to be the space to accommodate two cultures. The Aborigines still – understandably – hurt, but hopefully their voices will be heard at last.

9

Zambia

We flew to Zambia from Sydney, via Johannesburg. We bade a sad farewell to lovely Alex, who waved us off from the terminal. We sat in the coach saying how much we liked him and how we'd miss him. The coach stopped at traffic-lights. There was a banging on the door. We didn't have to miss him – he was back again. We'd left a case behind and he'd sprinted after the coach to get it back to us. After that there was no time to talk about Alex, we needed a full investigation into how something had been left behind – it made nonsense of our new foolproof 'list and number' system.

We arrived in Livingstone. Named, of course, after the explorer. I wished someone could have got the wrong end of the stick and called the town I Presume. Our hotel had a safari theme – by which I mean there were fibreglass rhinos all over the lawn, and once a day about five depressed-looking zebras would walk through the grounds, the Zambian equivalent of seaside donkeys.

We had lunch in an open-air restaurant by the pool. The others, who could talk about food all day, leaving very little time to discuss matters of real importance, like luggage, were ordering fish and steak and all as happy as Larry. I, as usual, could see nothing vegetarian on the menu but there's only so many times you can go off in a huff and eat a huge Toblerone. Seeing fried eggs on one bit of the menu, and chips on another, I made a huge creative culinary leap, and asked if it would be possible to have the double helix of lower-middle-class eating, egg and chips. I should have known. They always hate it when you mess with their menu. The waiter gave a sigh like a deflating Lilo and said he'd ask in the kitchen.

I'll skip the intervening chunks of time, when happy crew all around me tucked into prawns and chicken salad and giraffe burgers, and fast forward to the arrival of my meal. Some very pale fries, the thin, limp, bored sort, the Paris Hiltons of the fried potato, and next to them, two smashed-flat leathery-looking things – insoles possibly, or lumbago patches. I didn't want to eat them, and I didn't want to leave them, when they'd gone to not much of that trouble. I smuggled them back to my room, and then felt I couldn't put them in the wastepaper basket so I threw them out of my window in the middle of the night. I thought I heard a strangled cry in the distance, as if a depressed zebra had been hit on the rump by a bit of overcooked protein, but, hey, you can't worry about everything.

～ *Introduction* ～

The country now known as Zambia was first brought to the world's notice by the missionary David Livingstone's description of the Victoria Falls, which he visited in 1855. Squeezed into its present dumb-bell shape by the 1890s 'Scramble for Africa', between Britain, Portugal and Germany, Northern Rhodesia was administered by Cecil Rhodes's British South Africa Company until it became a British protectorate in 1924. After its failure to federate with Malawi and Southern Rhodesia, Northern Rhodesia became independent as the Republic of Zambia in 1964. With a prosperous and well-developed copper industry, Zambia was then the second-richest African country. Today it is one of the world's poorest, with an income per head of almost exactly one tenth that of its neighbour, Botswana, and half of what it had been as a British protectorate.

This disastrous collapse was due to the eccentric economic policies of the first president, Kenneth Kaunda, and his one-party state, and the corruption of his successor, Frederick Chiluba. Today, with a more realistic government, and the copper mines newly owned by Indian, Australian and Canadian enterprises, the eleven million Zambians expect a slow return to prosperity.

As we approached the dusty road leading towards the Makuni village, not far from Livingstone in Zambia, we reminded ourselves that on meeting Chief Makuni we would greet him on one knee, bow our heads and clap three times. Then we saw the chief speeding away in a car in the opposite direction. We were late and he had an appointment elsewhere.

A Zambian village is traditionally built in a semi-circle to protect the cattle. We could hear occasional chanting and shouts from behind the thatched perimeter wall but could see nothing until we turned into the entrance. Beyond the modern breezeblock buildings there were a number of round mud huts with conical thatched roofs. Several people were about, and children were playing, kicking clouds of dust into the air. Above the chatter we could hear birdsong in the surrounding trees. Every now and then a guided tour of twenty or thirty Western tourists walked through the village.

Two rows of Toka Leya tribeswomen lined our path, parallel to the compound wall. They wore bright red or black berets, black T-shirts and red kangas with a simple black-and-white design of symbolic shields and animals. We were led to the thatched round mud hut of the chieftainess, who would receive us in place of her father, we were told. We knelt and clapped three times before entering.

The chieftainess and the prime minister were seated in the dark interior and we were invited to sit on a wooden seat that ran along the wall. A throne with lions carved into the armrests was reserved for the chief, and a lion skin was spread on the ground. Although it was late afternoon and the hut was cooling, flies buzzed everywhere.

The chieftainess was tall and striking with high cheekbones, dressed in grey with a green-and-red patterned wrap, a shell necklace and a round flat-topped black hat draped with animal hide. She and the prime minister had honoured us in bringing us into this important hut, and welcomed us warmly to the village. As she led us outside, the sun was setting and the village was crowded. Cars were parked in the shade. Music floated out to us from bars where men stood at wooden counters with their beer.

A hundred years ago, the village had been very different. 'It's modernised,' explained the chieftainess. 'A long time ago, people didn't go to school so they were not able to write. Now we have a basic school that gives free education from pre-school to grade seven.' Tourism has become the village's main source of income: 'We depend on it,' she told us. 'We want more tourists to come here. Then people will sell what they make [beadwork and basketry] so they can afford to take their children to school, or buy food for themselves and their family. The money that tourism brings will be used to help the school and the clinic. The clinic is nearly finished so people who cannot afford the transport into town can have their blood tests here.'

She led us to a large spreading tree under which David Livingstone had been received by her ancestor, 'chief number thirteen'. We asked her whether anything about the lives of the Toka Leya people had improved after the British arrived in Zambia. The chieftainess was adamant that everyone in Zambia had benefited from their presence. Certainly the village seemed to be prospering and the traditional culture was kept alive, not just for the benefit of overseas visitors but for its own people. However much Western influences may intrude, the chief and chieftainess felt it important that the children of the tribe should remember their past.

∼ *A Human Explosion* ∼

Afrikaners sometimes claim defensively that their ancestors inhabited South Africa before the Blacks, and it is true that the indigenous inhabitants displaced by the Dutch after 1663, when the first colonists arrived at Cape Town, were Khoikhoi – Hottentots, or San – Bushmen. At that time the nearest black tribes were perhaps some two hundred miles or so to the east, but they were on the move.

For hundreds of years Bantu speakers had been migrating south, bringing with them agricultural techniques, iron tools and weapons, absorbing or displacing the original inhabitants, until in the eighteenth century they met advancing Dutch colonists. By the start of the nineteenth century, when the British took over the Cape of Good Hope, the frontier between black and white communities became vigorously contested. It was then that the human explosion of bloody forced migrations generally known as the '*mfecane*' erupted.

Nothing in modern history matches the violence and speed of the *mfecane*'s forced migrations. Six of today's African countries – Swaziland, Lesotho, Botswana, Zimbabwe, Malawi and Zambia – originated in that human torrent; perhaps the closest parallel in history is the flood of Alexander the Great's Macedonians in Asia and Egypt. It began with a banal quarrel, in what is now the South African province of KwaZulu-Natal, between three Ngoni leaders contending for regional supremacy – Zwide, Sobhuza and Dingiswayo. Sobhuza was the first to emigrate, taking his followers to what is now Swaziland, establishing a dynasty that still exists. Dingiswayo was defeated and killed in 1817,

*Naval officers had many dangerous tasks: Lieutenant Francis
Farewell negotiating with Shaka*

but was speedily avenged by his follower, Shaka, chief of a
then relatively small clan, the Zulu. Zwide was decisively
beaten by Shaka c.1819.

Historians argue the causes of the subsequent drama, but
Shaka's genius was an essential factor. Previous fights had
shown defects in organisation and weapons, which Shaka
radically changed. In so doing he altered the nature of
southern African societies. He was an absolute monarch: all
petty chiefdoms were abolished and authority given to
appointed officials who could be removed, usually permanently, at Shaka's pleasure. Warriors were remorselessly
drilled during a compulsory service that lasted for many

years. They fought in closely massed divisions, armed with long-bladed stabbing spears – the *assegai*. Once the enemy was engaged, the fight was to the death and almost always resulted in a Zulu victory.

Young men were formed into age-regiments, each supported by a herd of cattle, whose hides were used to make the regiments' distinctive shields. Similar numbers of girls formed non-combatant units, and married the men when their period of service was complete. A rear echelon of royal barrack towns was built, each governed by a female relation of Shaka's, where supplies of weapons were prepared and stored. Faced with what was, at that time, an

A Zulu warrior in parade dress

incomparable military machine, the only response was surrender or flight. Fugitives were pushed further on by the new Boer communities, themselves avoiding British jurisdiction. Some blacks sought British protection from the Boer rifles, which were even more deadly than the Zulu *assegais*, and formed states with a degree of self-government that have contrived to retain their independence for the best part of two centuries – Basutoland, now Lesotho, and Bechuanaland, now Botswana. Others dispersed more than a thousand miles eastwards, to Mozambique, or north across the Zambezi, or west to force more pressure on what became the British authority at the Cape. Shaka himself was assassinated by his brothers; his heir Dingane was defeated by the Afrikaners, and eventually the last Zulu monarch, Cetswayo, was forced – but only after a massive defeat at Ishandhlwala – to accept British sovereignty. He was received admiringly by Queen Victoria, who had been born in the year of Shaka's first victory.

～ Turbulent Times ～

Three streams of aggressive refugees, intent on carving out new territories, pushed north. Mzilikazi, who had been one of Shaka's best generals, rebelled around 1821 and led his people, the Ndebele, or Matabele, over the Drakensberg river where he established an autocratic kingdom along Zulu lines. Displaced by the Boers, they moved on across the Limpopo river, into what is now Zimbabwe, killing or pushing aside the native Shona and creating bitter animosities that still haunt that miserable country. On their western borders the Matabele were faced by the Tswana, also victims of the mfecane, who had trekked round the Kalahari Desert to reach the Zambezi; across the river the Kololo, a related Sotho people, had taken over the Lozi kingdom, with little violence.

Some of the former Ngoni people penetrated furthest north, some reaching the shores of Lake Victoria. Others remained near Lake Nyassa, now Lake Malawi, where they devastated and subdued the local tribes. The new Tswana, Kololo and Matabele states all met on the river, near the Victoria Falls: they had moved nearly two thousand miles from the *mfecane's* epicentre in a single generation.

Into this still-fluid and violent mix of African tribes, a

new influence was introduced. 'It requires some little patience to live quietly in these turbulent times,' wrote Mary Moffat, but she and her husband Robert spent fifty years at their mission station in Bechuanaland. In 1841 David Livingstone, who married their daughter and speedily pushed the mission northward into the tumult, joined them. He had been drawn away from the comparatively peaceful south by the itch to explore and a passionate loathing of the slave trade, which, deprived of its outlets on the west coast, was expanding in the east.

Livingstone's great journey, in which he crossed Africa from coast to coast between 1853 and 1856, made him the most famous man of his time. His book *Missionary Travels and Researches in South Africa* was not only an instant best-seller but accepted in the most scholarly institutions. Until

'Dr Livingstone, I presume?' H. M. Stanley meets Livingstone

his death in 1873, his continued travels, disappearance and 'rescue' by H. M. Stanley captivated the British public. One incident in particular shaped future British policies. In July 1871 Livingstone witnessed a massacre in which Swahili Arab slave traders killed at least four hundred people in a peaceful market; Livingstone himself snatched up a pistol, and managed to rescue some. His published account sparked the determination to end this disgraceful trade.

Livingstone's experiences convinced him that Africans could successfully face any challenges that the future might hold; his transcontinental journey had been made in co-operation with the Kololo, whose chief Sekelutu funded the expedition. It would probably not have succeeded without Livingstone's determination, but the extraordinary journey was essentially an African enterprise.

He believed that Africans must be assisted to counter the shock of the new, and equipped to resist 'tyrants and mur-derers' – that was his description of the Boers, but he was equally appalled by what he saw as the British authorities' oppression of the Xhosa in the Western Cape. He wrote, 'We are not advocates for war but we would prefer perpetual war to perpetual slavery. No nation ever secured its liberty with-out fighting for it. And every nation on earth worthy of its freedom is ready to shed its blood in its defence.' The 'true Negro family' was entitled to take its place in the 'general community of nations'. It was not a message that many Europeans wanted to hear.

The next morning we visited Livingstone, a colonial town whose main street is lined with houses that have corrugated-iron roofs and wide verandas that date back to the days of early British settlers. The town is being restored to provide tourist accommodation, and new hotels are springing up along the banks of the Zambezi.

A museum stands at the top of Constitution Hill and the main street was busy, with shops, banks and cafés, safari vehicles and buses. The only food available seemed to be in restaurants but a few people were selling little bowls of sweet potatoes at the roadside. When Livingstone was originally established in 1905, there were two towns, one for Europeans and one for Africans. Each had their own schools and hospital, but those for the Africans were more rudimentary. The Europeans – engineers, missionaries and hospital workers – lived at the top of the hill and never went into the African area where the Maramba market takes place today.

We were lucky to have met up with local journalist Luckson Nthani, who was keen to talk, show us around and encourage us to try some local produce, most of which is grown locally or found in the bush. We watched a woman preparing maize. 'They pound it, remove the chaff, then cook it, adding sugar or groundnuts,' Luckson explained. We walked through the teeming market where hundreds of ramshackle stalls, with canvas awnings supported on sticks, sold just about everything from root vegetables, grain and field produce to dry leaf tobacco, which you crush in your palm and roll in newspaper to smoke, and the local Viagra – a root that is boiled and the juice drunk. It tasted a bit like beetroot. It was intensely hot, dry and dusty, with clouds of flies that buzzed over the many dried-fish stalls. In an open area, people laid their wares, sometimes just a few vegetables, on a white cloth or a piece of sacking, with an umbrella as their only protection against the sun.

We were the only Europeans in the market but Luckson assured us that 'We have many white people who live in Livingstone in harmony with the blacks. In fact, there are even black and white marriages so now there are no restrictions in the town at all. The Maramba market is a tourist attraction so many white people come here with their guides.'

Towards the back of the market, we found a medicine man's stall under a wide-spreading tree. A table was covered with dried snakes, tortoiseshells, feathers and roots. The herbalist deals with medical and psychological problems, and told us about some of the more traditional cures: inhaling the smoke from burnt tortoiseshell to cure bleeding, python oil for earache, and roots as an analgesic. He noticed that we had come to his stand rather than to any of the other medicine stalls. We thought this was because his was nearest to the entrance but he assured us that we had been drawn there by a medicine he had mixed.

He showed us his remedy for people with business problems: 'He puts it on his face so that if a person comes to his business and looks at him, this person will feel an urge to buy things.' The most common problems he treated were haemorroids and sexually transmitted diseases. Although his cures may seem unorthodox to us, he maintains a close relationship with hospital doctors and refers to them what he cannot treat, such as HIV and AIDS cases. In return, they refer 'marriage problems' to him.

He also seen people who are 'possessed by evil spirits', an affliction he can alleviate. When asked where he learnt his trade, he replied: 'From God.'

∼ *We Have Got the Maxim Gun and They Have Not* ∼

In May 1889 the future of two African countries was decided in the Westminster Palace Hotel by Harry Johnston and Cecil Rhodes. Johnston – a junior consular officer, aged thirty-one, a drop-out from university and art-school – and Rhodes, a multi-millionaire, who was soon to become Prime Minister of the Cape colony, were an unlikely pair, but Johnston had attracted the attention of the British Prime minister, Lord Salisbury, and had even spent a weekend at Salisbury's home, Hatfield House, much to the chagrin of more senior Colonial Office staff. By contrast, Rhodes was more than a name to Lord Salisbury, 'a South African MP, rather a pro-Boer, I fancy'. Prompted by Salisbury, Johnston had written an article for *The Times* that set out an ambitious plan for a British Africa, which included a Cape–Cairo railway – a plan that matched Rhodes's own ideas.

Johnston and Rhodes had met for the first time at dinner the previous evening and had talked through the

Sir Harry Johnston; at home in the African bush or at Hatfield

night; at breakfast, Rhodes handed the other man a cheque for £2,000; at five in the afternoon, having banked the cheque, Johnston was in Lord Salisbury's office – nineteenth-century Prime Ministers were rather more accessible than those of today.

The deal agreed on that day in May was that Rhodes's newly founded British South Africa Company would be granted a royal charter that would enable it to enter into treaties with local chiefs in Zambezia, an extensive area north of the Limpopo. Rhodes's company was to bear all expenses, guaranteed by the illustrious name of Rothschild. The British government would pay only Johnston's expenses in the area around Lake Nyassa, where a British chartered company of a different kind, the African Lakes Company, had established a presence. Inspired by Livingstone, and supported by Scottish philanthropists, it operated steamers on Lake Nyassa and had founded a mission station at Blantyre. It would keep the religious folk happy, Lord Salisbury considered, if the area became a British protectorate. It was a remarkably small price to pay for control of what are now Zambia, Zimbabwe and Malawi.

The British South Africa Company, on paper thoroughly respectable, with two dukes on the board ('dummies and figureheads'), was little more than a vehicle for Rhodes's personal ambitions. Its first venture was to obtain the exclusive right to all mineral exploitation in Matabeleland, then controlled by Mzilikazi's successor, Lobengula, and to occupy the territory previously taken from the Shona. This was done without resistance, but proved disappointing. Mashonaland, the home of the ruins of Great Zimbabwe, was thought to be the mythical land of Ophir, rich in gold –

Cecil Rhodes in besieged Kimberley during the Anglo-Boer War

but none was found, and the expenses of occupation were crippling. Lobengula's own land had to be seized or the company would have been bankrupted.

The invasion of Matabeleland was a classic example of arrogant duplicity. Lobengula's men provided the excuse by killing hundreds of Shona just outside the British settlement of Fort Victoria. Although they harmed no Europeans, Rhodes felt justified in mounting a punitive expedition. A small mounted force – seven hundred troopers with five Maxim guns and two field-pieces – slaughtered thousands of Matabele. Lobengula and his chiefs escaped to commit suicide in the mountains, and white settlers, mainly British, flocked in to seize their lands. The new state, the size of Germany, became the British colony of Southern Rhodesia.

In 1898 the original Western pioneers established themselves about five kilometres from Victoria Falls in a settlement they called Old Drift or Sekuti's Drift. In the 1890s it was established as a crossing-point on the river for goods coming into central Africa from the Cape Colony. The village was at the shallowest point of the river so people could cross on foot. After a few crocodile attacks, a better way was found for Europeans to cross: on the shoulders of Africans. In 1900, the Reverend Giovanni Daniele Augusto Coisson, an Italian cleric, was sent to open a mission there. A contemporary account describes 'the mission station which Mr Coisson has entirely built and planned himself. It stands on the peninsula formed by the bend of the Zambezi, which flows behind it, though the front of the house is quite a little walk from the landing-stage. Within a stake fence stand a spacious church, a cottage with a veranda and a high-pitched thatched roof . . . another much smaller cottage . . . and three or four round huts.' For two years, Mrs Coisson was the only European woman living there.

Gradually the settlement grew as newcomers arrived to open shops, a hotel and bars, but they faced a serious problem: malaria. The disease claimed the lives of many, including the doctor and a couple of chemists. In the end, the railway was to decide the fate of the Old Drifters. In 1904 the line from Bulawayo reached the south bank of the Victoria Falls. As work began on the Maramba Bridge, it became clear that once the railway ran across the gorge, the crossing at Old Drift would become redundant. After ten years of living in the mosquito-infested swampland, the inhabitants were moved further upstream to the new settlement of Livingstone on Constitution Hill. Despite the discomforts of the area and frequent deaths from malaria, the settlers were reluctant to move. They were persuaded to do so by the British South African Company, who introduced fines for those who refused.

Today there is little to see at Old Drift except what remains of the cemetery with only the British names on the headstones as a reminder of the area's history. The site of the settlement has been subsumed into Mosi-oa-Tunya National Park, famous for being home to what may be Zambia's last white rhinos. When we drove through the park, we were accompanied by an armed and ever-watchful game warden. On our way out, we came across a couple of white rhinos lying under a tree about two hundred metres from us. The driver stopped and our warden took us on foot to within twenty metres of them. Both seemed to be fast asleep, their breath kicking up puffs of dust. They were huge. As we were about to leave, one lumbered to its feet and looked inquisitively in our direction. You could have heard our collective sharp intake of breath in Zimbabwe. Suddenly we felt a bit foolish to be standing just twenty metres away from a rhino that, clearly, we'd just disturbed. Would it charge?

'Look,' laughed the warden, who was as cool as a cucumber. 'He wants to come and say hello.'

We didn't stick around to find out if that was true.

～ *Some Distinguished Examples* ～

With Christopher Columbus and Simon Bolivar, Cecil Rhodes has given his name to a country – in fact to two,

Both Rhodesias have changed their names but Cecil Rhodes is gratefully remembered by thousands of Rhodes scholars

Northern and Southern Rhodesia. The British South Africa Company's acquisition of Northern Rhodesia was not accompanied by the violence that had characterised its aggression in the south: indeed, with a handful of troops in an area larger than France, Johnston was in no position to offer it. He had his work cut out to cope with the Nyassa protectorate. The largest native state, the Lozi kingdom of Barotseland, now Bulozi, also willingly accepted British protection.

Their king, Lewanika, had regained his land from the Kololo, Livingstone's old allies, and learnt the value of missionary protection. He had consulted his neighbour across the Zambezi, in Bechuanaland, by then also a British protectorate. Chief Khama of the Tswana assured Lewanika that the British, apart from their peculiar aversion to slavery, interfered little with his – admittedly prudent and tolerant – rule. Lewanika concurred, and appealed for British protection. This was eventually agreed in 1899, with some reluctance, and mainly to prevent the Portuguese expanding from Angola. Sovereignty over Barotseland was transferred from the Company to the Crown, and Khama's people survived to become independent Botswana, but the Lozi, although protected and secured in at least part of their former lands, never achieved the same status.

Close by, the mighty Victoria Falls roars into a deep gorge, boiling into the rapids below, in contrast to the wide, lazily flowing river above. However, we had arrived in the dry season so little water was tumbling into the gorge and the grooves in the massive rock walls lay exposed. The Falls are important to the Toka Leya people, who link them to the spirits of their ancestors. In the gorge, steps are carved to mark each chief who has gone before Chief Makuni, and offerings of bead necklaces and bracelets are tossed in to appease the malevolent deity believed to haunt them.

We couldn't leave without getting closer to the Falls, locally known as Mosi-oa-Tunya, 'the smoke that thunders', so that evening we took a boat on the river. As the sun dropped behind the horizon, leaving the clouds washed with gold, we were joined by a group of hippos that surfaced, took a brief look at us, then submerged again. They can stay under water for a considerable amount of time during which they change position, so catching them on film is a hit-or-miss affair – harder even than filming the dolphins in the Bay of Islands. As for the Falls, they were virtually silent but we saw drifts of spray that whirled up from the bottom of the gorge. Little about them would have changed since Livingstone became the first European to witness this scenery at sunset.

The following morning was overcast but still warm as we walked through the dusty bush, past dozens of monkeys to a vantage-point at the heart of the Falls where we would have an uninterrupted view of the railway bridge that spans the vertiginous gorge between Zambia and Zimbabwe. Completed in 1905, it was intended as a vital link in Cecil Rhodes's Cape–Cairo railway network.

Earlier that day we had chartered one of the original steam trains to run from the Zimbabwean town of Victoria Falls to Livingstone. It was plush inside, with comfortable padded wooden armchairs that faced each other across blue carpet, ceiling fans, and old pictures of railway life on the wood-panelled walls between the windows. The staff were smart in white suits, with red sashes and white topees.

At the viewing-point, we met Heather Chalcraft, from Lusaka, who edits the Zambian online magazine the *Low Down*. Her enthusiasm for Cecil Rhodes and the building of the railway bridge was infectious: 'There aren't many people who think, I'm just going to take a whole continent and turn it into part of my country.' After Oxford, Rhodes had come to South Africa to farm cotton, then moved up to the diamond fields in Kimberley, and to the Johannesburg area for gold. A dyed-in-the-wool imperialist, he would have liked to see the whole world under British rule. 'Rhodes had a vision of there being British colonies all the way from the Cape to Cairo. In terms of the railway, he almost made it. The final link was built in the 1970s when a railway link was completed from

Zambia to the port at Dar Es Salaam, in Tanzania. The great north road is virtually completed too.'

As we gazed at this extraordinary feat of engineering, Heather explained how it had been built: 'Rhodes wanted this bridge to link Zimbabwe with the copper mines in the Katanga province. He wanted the spray from the Falls to hit the railway carriages as they crossed. Sadly, he died in 1902, just three years before the bridge was completed. Designed by George Hobson and Ralph Freeman, it was built by the Cleveland Bridge Company in their UK yard, then shipped out here in kit form.' Construction was a huge enterprise, which involved shooting a rocket carrying a cable across the gorge so that the materials could be winched to the other side. A safety net was rigged up beneath the works until the men apparently said that it made them more nervous and asked for it to be removed. 'They employed thirty skilled workers and about two hundred local Africans, who took nineteen weeks to build the bridge out from either side of the gorge and join it in the middle. An amazing feat, thanks to Cecil Rhodes.

'Because he believed the English people were a superior race he isn't viewed as favourably as he might be, but, despite the unfavourable things, he had the most enormous vision for this continent. I often look at it and think, if we had carried on with that, Africa would be the most amazing place.'

∼ Neighbours, But Not Good Friends ∼

Zambia borders on seven countries: the Democratic Republic of Congo, Tanzania, Mozambique, Zimbabwe,

Namibia, Botswana and Angola. Some of the frontiers are reasonable – the Zambezi and the series of rivers and lakes that define the north-eastern provinces are natural boundaries – but most are arbitrary colonial definitions. The boundary between Zambia and what was then German East Africa, now Tanzania, entailed the most drastic adjustment. In 1807 the British had taken the small and insignificant North Sea island of Heligoland, five square miles in extent, from the Danes. In 1892 the German government thought it absolutely essential to them as a naval base: would Britain consider exchanging it for a hundred thousand square miles of East Africa? A rapid agreement secured Zambia's north-eastern borders, but the most extraordinary cartographical consequence of this deal was the creation of the Caprivi Strip that Germany retained. Named after the German Chancellor of the time, this three-hundred-mile corridor of land, barely thirty miles wide, sliced through Bechuanaland and Zambia in order to give access from German South West Africa/Namibia to the Zambezi. Quite useless for this purpose, the Strip now harbours one of Africa's least likely independence movements.

Belgium was a more difficult neighbour. The existence of massive and easily accessible copper deposits in Katanga was well known, and both Rhodes and King Leopold simultaneously despatched expeditions to the local king, Msiri. Four Belgian and two British parties attempted to obtain his support: the Belgians won by the simple expedient of killing the king, and the resulting compromise divided the Copper Belt between the Congo and Northern Rhodesia.

Portugal could claim to be Britain's oldest ally, but that did not help her ambitions in Africa. Controlling extensive colonies on the Atlantic and Indian Ocean coasts, the Portuguese wanted their share in the Scramble to consist of the bridge between Angola and Mozambique. This ambition was abruptly forestalled by the British occupation of Northern Rhodesia. Harry Johnston was already in residence in Zomba when a Portuguese army – seven hundred men, with modern rifles, a considerable force at that time – arrived in the protectorate. Lord Salisbury ordered them to withdraw. The public in Lisbon was furious: Portugal had just lost her former Brazilian empire. The Portuguese government resigned. Agreement was reached, then denounced, and another government elected before the Portuguese, with bad grace, knuckled under.

∼ You Never Heard of a Country Changing Its Name ∼

Rhodes succeeded in his grand design, but his career was cut short by a farcical raid into the Afrikaner Transvaal Republic by his lieutenant, Dr Leander Starr Jameson, in collusion – although this was strenuously denied at the time – with the British authorities, including the Colonial Secretary Joseph Chamberlain. The humiliating failure of the raid forced Rhodes to resign as Cape premier in 1895. 'They can't take it away from me, can they?' he asked anxiously. 'You never heard of a country changing its name.'

The name stayed until independence in 1964, and Rhodes's policies were not much altered. Even though the 1890s were afflicted by drought, locusts and cattle disease, Northern Rhodesia remained peaceful. New taxes caused protests, but there were no revolts. The rush of

European settlers to Southern Rhodesia – which proved the foundation of the country's prosperity and its political turmoil – was less marked in the north; even by 1911, when control passed from the Company to the High Commissioner for South Africa, there were no more than fifteen hundred European inhabitants. Zambia's wealth was to come from the copper industry.

In Africa, the first and now the last leg of our journey, we were confronted by thoughts about how determined and committed those who built the empire must have been. The Zambian landscape is dry and dusty for much of the year and, ostensibly, seems not to offer much. But profit was not the force that drove Livingstone across the continent to Victoria Falls. He was more interested in saving souls and suffered a great deal for his missionary zeal. Years later, it was the single-mindedness of Cecil Rhodes that connected Zambia to the outside world with his dream of a pan-African railway. What men, what vision, what a time.

Having completed our whistle-stop journey round the globe, we found it hard to draw any firm conclusions about the British, their ambitions, achievements and failures. Each country had told its own story, which cast the British in both good and bad lights. Rather than a determined effort by the British government to scatter its ambassadors and generals across the globe to wrest countries from those who already lived there, the empire had been built gradually, over about three hundred years. In some cases guile was employed to tease land from the locals; in others, it was wrenched away with unmatchable force. But in all cases, with the partial exception of Australia, the incentive that drove powerful men to leave their homes and venture into unmapped, often dangerous lands was the acquisition of wealth. And it seems to be part of the human condition that when huge amounts of money are involved there are winners and losers – which begs the question, why, in the period that the British Empire was emerging, were so many winners born and bred in Britain?

It's hard to sum up the effect of Empire in these countries. The West Africans transported to Jamaica experienced the worst treatment that the British could mete out. But their descendants, modern Jamaicans, show a strength of spirit you might not expect to find in a people with such a tragic past.

India was dominated by the British, yet it was the British who unified the subcontinent, and India's use of the English language is of key importance to its global economic growth.

In Hong Kong the symbiotic relationship between the Chinese work ethic and British law led to the tiny island's financial success story.

The British education system is highly regarded in Borneo, and many Canadians, Australians New Zealanders are still keen to Elizabeth II as their monarch.

In Britain, now, many of us can admit to a creeping sense of shame about the darker side of our forefathers' achievements. And it is right to feel so about many events. But to feel shame alone is wrong. The British men and women who felt an undeniable urge to explore the world, seeking new opportunities, went into the unknown with a courage and determination rarely seen today. It was an extraordinary time when the world was changed and the great story of the British Empire was written.

A Final Word

The big, spectacular finish to our journey was Victoria Falls. I didn't like to say anything, but it wasn't quite the torrent I had seen on the fridge magnets. Pouring over the edge was a single stream of water – like a bath tap. There was nothing to say. It had been in full spate when the researcher had been to recce, and now it wasn't.

I stood by the rail and tried to summon up some kind of conclusion, but there couldn't be one, really. The Empire is a big amorphous mass, part history, part branding, part fond memory. Some bits of the journey were fascinating, and some were like going to a museum with no gift shop. I felt the terrible burden of trying to react to it all, to have some sort of emotion. The whole thing had been a bit like trying to take a plate of blancmange up a loft ladder without a plate – and I suppose it didn't matter that bits fell off along the way. I looked over the gorge. Victoria Falls. If I fell off along the way it would be bad news for me, but at least it wouldn't take them long to think of a headline.

Further Reading

General

Oxford History of the British Empire (four volumes) (OHBE) (Oxford, 1998–2003)

Denis Judd; *Empire: The British Imperial Experience from 1765* (London, 1996)

David Cannadine; *Orientalism: How the British Saw their Empire* (London, 2003)

Niall Ferguson; *Empire: How Britain Made the Modern World* (London, 2004)

David S. Landes; *The Wealth and Poverty of Nations* (London and New York, 1998)

Ghana and Slavery

Hugh Thomas; *The Slave Trade* (London, 1997)

C.R. Boxer; *The Portuguese Seaborne Empire* (London, 1973)

R. Law; *The Slave Coast of West Africa* (Oxford, 1991)

Trevor R. Getz; *Slavery and Reform in West Africa* (Oxford, 2004)

Adam Hochschild; *Bury the Chains: The British Struggle to Abolish Slavery* (Basingstoke, 2006)

D. Nicol (ed); *Africanus Horton: The Dawn of Nationalism in Modern Africa* (London, 1969)

Jamaica

Catherine Hall; *Civilising Subjects* (Cambridge, 2002)

J.R. West; *British West Indies in the Age of Abolition* (OHBE) vol. 2. (Oxford, 1998)

Richard Sheridan; *The Formation of Caribbean Plantation Society* OHBE, vol. 2 (Oxford, 1998)

J.H. Parry; *Trade & Dominion: European Overseas Empires in the Eighteenth Century* (London, 1974)

Newfoundland

O.P. Dickason; *Canada's First Nations* (Oxford, 1998)

Beth La Dow; *The Medicine Line, Ontario 2002* (New York & London, 2002)

Samuel Eliot Morison; *The European Discovery of America: The Northern Voyages* (New York, 1971)

G. Martin; Chapter 23 in *OHBE*, vol 3 (Oxford, 1999)

India

Abraham Evaly; *The Mughal Throne* (London, 2003)

Percival Spear; *A History of India* (London, 1965)

Ramachandra Guha; *A Corner of a Foreign Field, the Indian History of a British Sport* (Basingstoke, 2002)

Philip Mason; *A Matter of Honour: an Account of the Indian Army* (London, 1974)

D.A. Washbrook & R.J. Moore; Chaps 18 and 19, *OHBE* vol. 3 (Oxford, 1999)

Hong Kong

Frank Welsh; *A History of Hong Kong* (London, 1998)

J.K. Fairbank; *Trade & Diplomacy on the China Coast* (Stanford, 1964)

Ronald Hyam; *Empire and Sexuality* (Manchester, 1990)

Elizabeth Sinn; *Power & Charity: the Early History of the Tung Wah Hospital* (Hong Kong, 1989)

Chan Lau Kit-ching; *China, Britain and Hong Kong*

1895–1995 (Hong Kong, 1990)

Borneo

Anthony Reid; *Charting the Shape of Early Modern Southeast Asia* (Bangkok, 1993)

K.G. Tregonning; *Under Chartered Company Rule* (Singapore, 1958)

New Zealand

Michael King; *The Penguin History of New Zealand* (Auckland, 2003)

James Belich; *Paradise Reforged* (London, Melbourne 2001); *The New Zealand Wars* (1986)

David Denoon and Philippa Mein-Smith; *A History of Australia, New Zealand and the Pacific* (Oxford, 2000)

Australia

Frank Welsh; *Great Southern Land* (London, 2003)

David Goldsworthy (ed); *Facing North: A Century of Australian Engagement with Asia* (Melbourne, 2001)

Robert Hughes; *The Fatal Shore* (London, 1996)

David Day; *Claiming a Continent* (Sydney, 1997)

Henry Reynolds; *Aboriginal Sovereignty* (St Leonards, 1997)

Zambia

Basil Davidson; *The African Past: Chronicles from Antiquity to Modern Times* (London, 1966)

Andrew Ross; *David Livingstone: Mission and Empire* (London, 2002)

Thomas Pakenham; *The Scramble for Africa* (London, 1991)

Robert Guest; *The Shackled Continent- Africa's Past, Present and Future* (London, 2004)

Shula Marks; 'Southern and Central Africa, 1886–1910' in *The Cambridge History of Africa*, vol.6 (Cambridge, 1985)

Acknowledgements

The Producers would like to thank the production team and all those whose contributions have made this book possible, in particular Victoria Wood, Frank Welsh and Fanny Blake; director and photographer Ben Warwick; Jamie Munro, Lisa Perrin, Paul Sommers, Sonia Beldom, Holly Wintgens, Simon Arnold (and for his additional photography), Rebecca Harris, Veronica Turnbull and Jenny Spearing at Tiger Aspect; Nick Davies, Rowena Webb, Nicola Doherty and Kevin Stewart at Hodder & Stoughton; Lucy Ansbro at Phil McIntyre Associates; and Gordon Wise at Curtis Brown.

Illustration Credits

Bridgeman Art Library: 1, 5, 12, 15 (Wilberforce House, Hull City Museums and Art Galleries), 27 (Bibliothèque des Arts Décoratifs, Paris), 40, 46, 59, 96, 108 (Courtesy of the Council, National Army Museum, London), 158 (National Portrait Gallery, London), 183; Corbis: 177; Empics: 148; Getty Images: 268; Heritage Image Partnership: 141, 166 (British Library); Illustrated London News Picture Library: 29, 31, 120, 242, 259; Mary Evans Picture Library: 38, 57, 68, 69, 71, 86, 93, 97, 112, 128, 134, 143, 160, 165, 185, 188, 201, 222, 225, 229, 235, 241, 247, 256, 257, 265; National Archives of Canada, Ottowa: 67; National Portrait Gallery, London:

263; Courtesy Frank Welsh: 101.

Endpapers: Map of the World, showing the British Empire, 1901, anonymous colour lithograph. (Private collection/Ken Welsh/Bridgeman Art Library).